DR. AMRUTUR VENKATACHAR SRINIVASAN was born in India in the village of Amrutur, Kunigal Taluk, in India's southern state of Karnataka. He had eight years of formal education in Sanskrit, the liturgical language of Hinduism, followed by many years in the U.S. performing a wide variety of Hindu religious ceremonies of worship, weddings and housewarmings.

He is a popular writer and speaker, and has published and presented numerous papers on a variety of cultural, social and religious issues in the U.S. and India. He has given courses on India's epic literature at the University of Connecticut and Wesleyan University. A founding member of the Connecticut Valley Hindu Temple Society in 1979, he also established the Raga Club of Connecticut in 2006.

His publication, *The Vedic Wedding: Origins, Tradition and Practice*, (Periplus Line LLC, 2006, www.periplusbooks.com) is widely acclaimed and won the USA Book News 2007 Best Book Award in the category of Eastern Religions. He has developed a contemporary format for Vedic (Hindu) weddings which retains all essential Vedic rites within a one to two hour ceremony, and in practice has blended this approach with those of other creeds in many interfaith weddings. For additional details please visit www.indianweddings.us.com

Dr. Srinivasan's most recent publications include *The Bhagavad Gita: A Thread through the Eighteen Gems (2015)* and *Hinduism for Dummies* (2011). See http://www.voutube.com/watch?v=4tfJbxmBMYo (Preview)

~

Other Books by the Author

~

The Bhagavad Gita: A Thread through the Eighteen Gems
Periplus Line LLC, 2015

~

Hindu Engagement Ceremony: *The Workbook* (ebook), 2013

~

Hindu Wedding: The Workbook (ebook), 2013

~

Dharma: Hindu Approach to a Purposeful Life (ebook), 2013

~

Hinduism for Dummies, Wiley Publications, 2011

~

Hindu Wedding: The Guide, White River Press, 2010

~

Vedic Wedding: Origins, Tradition and Practice
Periplus Line LLC, 2006

~

How to Conduct Puja (set of 9)
Periplus Line LLC, 1999-2014

~

How to Conduct Seemantam: Hindu Rites for the Wellbeing of the Mother-To-Be
Periplus Line LLC, 2009.

Yaksha Prashna

~

Yudhishthira's Dialogue with Yama

यक्ष प्रश्न

A fable of wisdom and inspiration from the *Mahabharata* retold and translated into English, with Sanskrit text and transliteration, by

A. V. Srinivasan

www.visionbooksindia.com

Earlier Published in 1984, 2002 & 2014 in USA
Revised Editon Published by Vision Books, 2016
Reprinted 2024

ISBN 10: 81-7094-967-X
ISBN 13: 978-81-7094-967-1

Illustrations by Bapu; and K.S. Design Studio

Published by
Vision Books Pvt. Ltd.
(Incorporating Orient Paperbacks and CARING imprints)
24 Feroze Gandhi Road, Lajpat Nagar 3
New Delhi 110024, India.
Phone: (+91-11) 2984 0821 / 22
e-mail: visionbooks@gmail.com

Printed at
Ashim Print Line
38/2, 35 & 36 Sahibabad Industrial Area, Ghaziabad
Uttar Pradesh 201010, India.

Dedication

To
Amrutur,
my village in Karnataka.

~

Contents

Kamla

Preface

The ancient Indian epic, the *Mahabharata*, was composed in Sanskrit over thousands of years ago, and many versions have flourished over the centuries in other Indian languages. The Critical Edition published by the Bhandarkar Oriental Research Institute in Pune contains 18 sets of shlokas that pertain to the dialogue of questions and answers between the Yaksha and Yudhishthira and they are all included here. In other sources I have referred to and used earlier and here, there are 34 sets of such shlokas. In the current edition, for the sake of completeness, I have included all riddles and arranged them in the order in which they appear in the Aranya section of the *Aranya Parva* of the epic. We have also included some illustrations and made, where necessary, additions and revisions.

A. V. SRINIVASAN

June 2016

Yaksha Prashna

The Fable

This story is found in the *Aranya Parva* (The Forest Section) of the great Indian epic, the *Mahabharata.* The sons of Pandu along with their wife Draupadi are nearing the end of their twelve-year forest exile. They are due to begin the thirteenth and final year, which they are required to spend incognito. Were they to be discovered, their cycle of exile would begin all over again.

One day an agnihotri brahmin came rushing to the Pandavas and begged for help.

In ancient days it was the practice of certain brahmins to do homa and havana as a part of their daily rituals and worship. Fire is an essential part of most of such rituals. So, one of the tools needed in this practice is a device that can generate fire. In those days such a device consisted of two wooden pieces, a rod and a bow, the latter producing a churning action of the rod supported by a firm base of stone or wood. The churning action results in friction and heat at the support and any

The Mahabharata

The Sanskrit epic, the *Mahabharata*, is the longest poem in the world, having over 100,000 shlokas. This work is fifteen times the length of the Bible and eight times the length of the *Iliad* and *Odyssey* combined. It is a tale of jealousy and rivalry between royal cousins of the Kuru race, the Kauravas and the Pandavas. This no-holds-barred epic has everything: a cruel play of love, hatred, jealousy, greed, passion, violence, scandals, cheating, the hell of war and its aftermath, political intrigue, but also extraordinary kindness, duty, courage, decency, and more!

The Kuru kingdom was ruled by Shantanu. Shantanu's eldest son and logical heir Bhishma swore never to marry. So the royal lineage depended on the two surviving grandsons of Shantanu, descended from Shantanu's second marriage. Dhritarashtra, who was born blind, in turn had one hundred sons known as Kauravas. The eldest two of these were Duryodhana and Dushasana. Dhritarashtra's brother Pandu had five sons: Yudhishthira, Bhima, Arjuna, Nakula, and Sahadeva born through the agency of five boons given to his wife Kunti.

Bhishma appointed a famous expert in warfare, Dronacharya, to teach all the Kaurava and Pandava boys. The Pandava princes learnt well and met all challenges, excelling in each test of physical strength, endurance, and accuracy. They grew up to be intelligent, active, excelling in sports and loved by all. Among the five, the young Arjuna stood apart.

The Kauravas were a jealous lot, always suspicious of their cousins and afraid they might lay claim to the throne occupied by their blind father after Pandu's death. The Pandavas did rule well and wisely and grew in power. The seeds of jealousy that were sown in the boys' teens grew into a huge poisonous tree that is the *Mahabharata*.

The Kauravas began scheming and, with the active help from their uncle Shakuni, a game of dice was set up between the Kauravas and the Pandavas. The stakes began with jewels, gold, stables, elephants, cows, Yudhishthira's army, his treasury . . . and grew higher and higher until, in desperation and to the shouts of protest from the assembled elders, Yudhishthira staked and lost Sahadeva, his

(Contd . . .)

youngest brother. Brother after brother was staked as though they were chattel, and each was lost. Then Yudhishthira staked himself and again lost. The Pandavas were then the slaves of the Kauravas!

One would think this sad state of affairs had reached a climax, but not so – not yet!

Yudhishthira was next persuaded to stake his wife Draupadi under the condition that should he win, the Kauravas would go into forest exile for twelve years and spend the thirteenth year incognito. If they were to be discovered during that thirteenth year, they agreed to repeat the cycle. But if the Kauravas win, the Pandavas would do the same.

Yudhishthira goes along — and loses! The Pandavas had now lost everything and are banished to the forests for a long twelve years. Their life and adventure during this period of forest exile are narrated in the *Aranya Parva*, and the Yaksha Prashna fable is set therein. To conclude the story, the Pandavas succeeded in living disguised during the thirteenth year. Upon their return to the kingdom they were told that they would not get even five villages, let alone their rightful part of the empire.

With this sordid background the armies from each side assembled to fight a terrible war at a location known as Kurukshetra close to today's New Delhi, the capital of India. The armies are all in battle formation with horses and elephants and a variety of arms, medics, and so on. As the battle is about to begin, Arjuna loses heart and declares that he had no interest in fighting a battle in which he has to kill his elders, relatives, friends, and teachers. In despair, he throws his bow down from the chariot. At this fraught juncture, Lord Krishna teaches him the concept of dharma. That lesson taught on a battlefield is the most sacred scripture of the Hindus — *The Bhagavadgita.*

The terrible and bloody battle that followed was finally won by the Pandava side. The principal Kaurava kings, their teacher Drona, their supporters were all killed. The blind king was still alive but Bhishma died. Dharma had been protected!

The Pandavas were crowned and ruled justly for a number of years before they relinquished the kingdom and retired. Arjuna's grandson Parikshit ascended the throne as the Dwapara Yuga was drawing to reach its end.

fibrous material at the base of the support catches fire, ready for use in a ritual.

Now, this brahmin had hung the fire-drilling sticks in a tree. A passing stag happened to stop by and rub its body against the trunk of this tree and in the process the sticks got entangled in the deer's articulated horns. The stag fled, struggling in vain to rid himself of this unwanted burden; but the more it shook its head, the more firmly did the fire sticks get wedged in its antlers. The distraught brahmin now wanted the Pandavas to pursue the fleeing animal and recover his sticks.

Being kshatriyas, the Pandavas held it as their duty to provide all help and protection to those who practiced their dharma. Therefore, the five Pandavas proceeded forthwith, fully armed, in pursuit of the stag. While they soon caught sight of the stag, their attempts to stop the animal failed and they were left tired by all the running and exertion. Not only had the quest failed, they ended up hungry, thirsty, angry and frustrated.

Finally the brothers sat down to rest under the cool shade of a large tree, fretting over the outcome of the relatively simple, uncomplicated task. Greater battles with their cousins lay ahead of them and yet they had not been able to help a brahmin even in such a simple matter.

Hot and thirsty, Yudhishthira, the eldest of the Pandava brothers, instructed Nakula to climb a tree in order to locate some nearby source of water so that they could quench their thirst. Nakula did so and saw a cluster of trees not too far off. He told Yudhishthira that he could hear the cries of water cranes from that direction, suggesting the presence of water. Yudhishthira asked Nakula to go to the pond and fetch some water in a quiver.

After walking a short distance, Nakula located a beautiful spot; a crystal clear lake, surrounded by trees, flowers and birds. Nakula was overjoyed. His first instinct was to enjoy a cool drink himself, as he was already there, and then carry water back for his brothers. So he descended to the water's edge. As he was about to scoop up some refreshing water, he heard a strong and clear voice of warning:

> मा तात साहसं कार्शीर्मम पूर्वपरिग्रहः
> प्रश्नानुक्त्वा तु माद्रेय पिबस्व च हरस्व च
>
> *mā tāta sāhasam, karśirmama pūrva parigraha:*
> *praśnānuktvā tu mādrēya pibasva ca harasva ca*
>
> O son of Madri, mine is the first prerogative. Do not dare to touch that water. You must first answer my questions and then you may drink it and (also) take it (for your brothers).

Nakula ignored the warning, drank some water — and immediately fell dead.

When Nakula did not return within a reasonable time, Yudhishthira suggested that Sahadeva go and take a look at what was delaying their brother. Sahadeva arrived on the scene and was shocked to see Nakula lying as though in deep asleep. But before investigating any further, he too sought to first quench his raging thirst. Sahadeva heard the same warning that Nakula had, ignored it as Nakula had, and, upon attempting to drink some water, also fell dead.

Dharma

If there is one word that is unique to Hinduism and is invoked when appropriate by Hindus — from a peasant to a prime minister — it has to be the word dharma. Every Hindu "knows" the word and its implications. The word dharma is formed from the root *dhr* and literally means to hold, sustain and maintain a thing in its being, leading to harmony and balance in nature.

Dharma is the moral law combined with spiritual discipline that guides both universal and individual life. The ancient Hindus considered dharma as the very foundation of one's life. पृथिवीं धर्मणा धृतं (*prthiveem dharmana dhrtam*) — The earth is upheld by dharma declares the *Atharva Veda* (XII – 1.17).

We may get a glimpse of its vast scope by translating dharma as right action, right conduct, virtue, moral law, ethical values, etc.

Every form of life, and every group of people — and, indeed, each individual has its dharma, which is the law of its being.

Dharma or virtue is conformity with the truth of things; adharma or vice is its opposite. Unfortunately, no single word in the English language adequately covers the meaning of dharma. Even the Sanskrit literature on the subject includes cryptic statements that aren't all that helpful beyond shedding a little light on how Hindu ancestors viewed this concept. Consider, for example, the following statements:

> धर्मेण हीनः पशुभिः समानः
> *Dharmena heenaha pashubhi samaanaha*
> The one devoid of dharma is an animal.

(Contd . . .)

अहिंसा परमो धर्म:
Ahimsa paramo dharmaha
Non-violence is the supreme dharma.

यतो धर्म: ततो जया:
Yato dharmah tato jayaaha
Where there is dharma, there is victory.

Additional descriptions of dharma include:

- "any matter enjoined by the Vedas with a view to attain any useful purpose,"
- "belief in the conservation of moral values,"
- "a mode of life or a code of conduct which regulates a man's work and activities as a member of society and as an individual to bring about his gradual development and enable him to reach what was deemed to be the goal of human existence,"
- "that which holds a thing together, makes it what it is, prevents it from breaking up and changing into something else . . . , its fundamental attribute, its essential nature, the law of its being,"
- "the code of life based on Vedas, the due observance of which leads to happiness here and hereafter," and
- "that scheme or code of laws which bind together human beings in the bonds of mutual rights and duties, of causes-and-consequences of actions arising out of their temperamental characters, in relation to each other and society," etc.*

These statements amply illustrate how dharma is central to the Hindu view of life.

---

* For a detailed discussion of these definitions and related discussion, see *On the Meaning of the Mahabharata* by V.S. Sukhtankar, The Asiatic Society of Bombay, 1957, pp. 79-83.

Now it was Arjuna's turn to investigate what was going on. He proceeded with his famed *Gandiva* bow in his hand, suspecting some trouble. Upon arriving at the lake he was stunned to see his two brothers lying apparently dead. He, too, first tried to quench his thirst and heard the same warning. Unlike Nakula and Sahadeva, Arjuna did not ignore the warning. Instead, he challenged the being to show itself and shot several arrows in the direction from which the voice came. The result was only a sterner warning. Whereupon the warrior Arjuna dared the voice by saying, "Stop me if you can," proceeded to drink the water, and fell down dead.

A short time later, Bhima arrived and met the same fate.

Now Yudhishthira was clearly worried. Wondering about the possibilities of harm befalling his dear and powerful brothers, he decided to go and look for them himself. When he arrived at the lake, he could not believe the dreadful sight that met his eyes. All four of his beloved brothers lay seemingly dead on the ground! Yudhishthira sat down beside them and lamented. All his hopes for the future now seemed shattered. How would he ever be able to recover his lost kingdom without the help of his able, powerful brothers? He grieved for a while and then began to look around to determine the reason for their deaths. He said to himself:

नैशां शस्त्र प्रहारोऽस्ति पदम् नेहास्ति कस्यचित्
भूतं महदिदं मन्ये भ्रातरो येन मे हतः

naiṣāṁ śastraprahāro'sti padaṁ nehāsti kasya cit
bhutaṁ mahadidaṁ manye bhrātaro yena me hatāḥ

There are no signs of violence upon their bodies, no foot prints anywhere. The killer must be a supernatural being.

He wondered if his malevolent cousin Duryodhana had had the pool poisoned but ruled it out because the faces of his brothers looked calm and serene. Convincing himself that it must have been some supernatural being, he approached the water's edge to drink some water. Then he, too, heard a stern voice:

अहं बकः शैवलमत्स्यभक्षो मया नीताः प्रेतवशं
तवानुजाः त्वं पञ्चमो भविता राजपुत्र
न चेत्प्रश्नान्पृच्छतो व्याकरोशि

ahaṁ bakaḥ śaivalamatsyabhakṣo mayā nītāḥ pretavaśaṁ
tavānujāḥ tvaṁ pañcamo bhavitā rājaputra
na cet praśnān pṛcchato vyākaroṣi

I am a crane living on moss and fish and the cause of your brothers' death. You shall be the fifth victim if you do not answer my questions.

Yudhishthira asked, "Who are you? Are you rudra, vasu, or marut? You must be very strong to have been able to put to death these powerful brothers of mine. Your feat is remarkable because no gods, antigods, gandharvas or rakshasas could

Yudhishthira, the Dharmaraja

Yudhishthira is the eldest among the five sons brought up by Queen Kunti and King Pandu. He was born to Kunti with god Dharma as his divine father – hence the two other names by which he is also known: Dharmaputra or Dharmaraja.

Name a quality that defines a noble prince and you find it in Yudhishthira. He was brave, kind, compassionate, patient, respectful of elders, affectionate with his equals and subjects, learned, skilful in warfare, . . .

But this noble and poised prince had one weakness. He loved to gamble. This single fault triggers a series of events in the Kuru kingdom that almost destroy the royal lineage in the Mahabharata war. After long years of trials and hardship — Yaksha Prashna is one such trial — he leads his brothers to war against his Kuru cousins and wins. Due to his righteous conduct, his personality remains intact and after several years as emperor of India, he relinquishes the throne, crowns the only surviving Pandava prince Parikshit, grandson of his brother Arjuna, and proceeds to the Himalayas and beyond. In this long and treacherous journey in the mountains, his wife Draupadi and one brother after another succumb and die. Only Yudhishthira followed by a loyal dog continues and arrives at the gates of heaven. God Indra receives the noble king and asks him to mount his chariot declaring that owing to his steadfastness to dharma he will be the first ever human to enter heaven alive!

Yudhishthira agrees to do so — along with the loyal dog that has stayed with him to the very last step! No amount of persuasion or threat can convince Yudhishthira to abandon the dog. Indra gives up and allows them in — only to find that the dog was none other than Yudhishthira's divine father, god Dharma! The last test is over and Yudhishthira enters heaven.

The brilliant phrase, *Dharmo Rakshati Rakshitaha* — those who protect dharma are protected by it — which encapsulates in one single compact statement all of Hindu philosophy is attributed to the noble Yudhishthira.

stand up to my brothers. But why did you kill them? What do you want, noble one? Why are you here? Who are you?"

The voice replied: "I am a Yaksha, Yudhishthira. May you prosper."

As he heard these words, Yudhishthira saw a form manifesting before his eyes. It had a massive, tall body with grotesque eyes, burning like the fire of the sun, and with a voice like thunder. "I warned your brothers. But they would not listen to me. So now they are dead. This pool belongs to me and unless you answer my questions you shall not even touch its water."

Whereupon Yudhishthira replied:

नचाहं कामये यक्ष तवपूर्वपरिग्रहं
यथाप्रज्नं तु ते प्रश्नान् प्रतिवक्ष्यामि पृच्छ मां

na cāham kāmaye yakṣa tava pūrva parigrahaṁ
yathā prajnam tu te praśnān prativakṣyāmi pṛccha māṁ

I have no desire to take what is yours, Yaksha.
Ask me and I will answer as best as I can.

Thus began Dharmaraja's* attempt to answer the Yaksha's questions.

---

* Literally, the King of Dharma; another name of Yudhishthira, the eldest of the Pandavas.

The Yaksha's questions and Yudhishthira's replies are beautiful, subtle, deep and with layers of meaning. Through Yudhishthira, Ved Vyasa has distilled the entire philosophy of Vedic Hindus into an enquiry comprising of some thirty-four sets of one hundred and twenty-two questions. The questions cover a vast canvas, jumping from one topic to another. These questions and their answers lay a firm framework for the gems of wisdom that are to come later in the epic as the teachings of *Srimad Bhagavadgita.* These questions and their answers are as important, as relevant and as significant today as they were when Yudhishthira stood by the side of his dead brothers, with his palms joined together, and attempted to meet the Yaksha's challenge.

The essence of Yudhishthira's answers have guided the lives of Hindus for centuries. They serve as torchlights that lead us from darkness, give us peace and comfort at times of stress, and guide us when faced with ethical dilemmas. These questions and answers have long been talked about, meditated and debated as successive generations have re-discovered the timeless beauty and truth of Vedic philosophy. Their message can inspire us to stand firm and tall and shape our lives towards excellence and truth.

The Test Begins

Says Yudhishthira:

. . . पृच्छ माम्

. . . *pṛccha mām*

. . . ask me

Asks the Yaksha:	***Yudhishthira replies:***
किं स्विदादित्यमुन्नयति केच तस्याभितश्चरितः कश्चैनमस्तं नयति कस्मिंश्च प्रतितिष्ठति	ब्रह्मादित्यमुन्नयति देवास्तस्याभितश्चराः धर्मश्चास्तम्नयति च सत्ये च प्रतितिष्ठति
kiṁ svidādityamunnayati *keca tasyābhitaścaritaḥ* *kaścainamastam nayati* *kasminśca pratitiṣṭhati*	*brahmādityamunnayati* *devāstasyābhitaścarāḥ* *dharmaścāstamnayati ca* *satye ca pratitiṣṭhati*
What makes the sun rise? Who moves around him? What causes the sun to set? In what is he established?	Brahma. Gods. Dharma. Truth.

This riddle has four parts. All center on the sun, referred to here as Aditya, the son of Aditi, the celestial mother of the Vedic gods. The facts given are: the sun rises, the sun sets; entities move around it; it is held firmly (up in the sky).

And, the Yaksha's question is: What causes these motions and positions?

There are two interpretations to the word "sun" here. One sees the sun (āditya) as the natural wonder, the life giving center of our world system and a principal creation of Brahma; the other interprets the sun to be one's inner light (ātma jyoti).

The sun is perhaps the earliest natural force worshipped by ancient Hindus and many other cultures. Science has established that the sun is central to the solar system of which the earth is a part. The sun's unfailing, regular and periodical "rising" and "setting" is based on our observations made from earth. This is a natural phenomenon occurring entirely due to the dynamics of systems in motion around the sun. Since ancient times, Hindus worship the sun and wind, water, fire, etc., and the heavenly bodies that orbit the sun as the Navagrahas, literally "nine planets." One may deduce that a natural balance that holds the universe together in a stable condition occurs when all these forces of nature are in harmony.

Yudhishthira's answers elevate the discussion to the most fundamental belief of Hindus, namely that Brahman, the all-inclusive, the eternal, the One without a second, is indeed the force behind all phenomena, including the phenomenon of the "rising" of the sun that sustains life on earth.

Yudhishthira's answer to the sun's "setting" reveals that the sun referred to here is one's own inner light — the atman. The setting, in that context, refers to the atman resolving itself as the Brahman — and not confusing itself as being its real home to be the body in which it now resides.

The sun and the atman are firmly fixed in their respective truths. The sun is held in space by the physical laws of gravitation, energy and motion — by evident truths. The atma jyoti is sustained by the timeless Absolute Truth.

Brahman and Atman

The world that we see with our eyes is dynamic. The sun rises and sets. So does the moon. Human and other beings are born, live, and die. In one's life time, even neighborhoods may change, decay, and be replaced. So a question ancient Hindus focused on was: **Does anything remain the same, forever,** through cycles of time when the world comes to an end only to be renewed later to begin the next cycle? The answer the rishis provided was a definite "Yes." The entity that is real, they said, is **Brahman.** At a fundamental level, the Hindu view is that God = Brahman.

One stated Hindu goal of life, is for the individual soul (atman), that resides in a body, to merge upon death with the Supreme Soul (Paramatman).

The sun in all its phases, rising, setting or fixed in space, recalls the rising within us of the ātma jyoti. The natural laws governing time and the heavenly bodies serve here as an illustration for the moral law, dharma.

Asks the Yaksha:	***Yudhishthira replies:***
केन स्विच्छ्रोत्रियो भवति	श्रुतेन श्रोत्रियो भवति
केन स्विद्विन्दते महत्	तपसा विंदते महत्
केन द्वितीयवान् भवति	धृत्या द्वितीयवान्भवति
केन च बुद्धिमान्	बुद्धिमान्वृद्धसेवया
kena sviccrotriyo bhavati	*śrutena*
kenasvid vindatemahat	*tapasā*
kena dvitīyavān bhavati	*dhṛtyā*
kena ca buddhimān	*vṛddhasevayā*
How does one become a scholar?	By studying the Vedas.
How does one become exalted?	Through tapas.
How does one gain a second self?	With resolve.
How does one become wise?	By serving the elders.

~

Ancient Hindus placed the utmost emphasis on acquiring spiritual knowledge. That inevitably meant a study of the Vedas, the four sacred books that serve as the foundation of Hinduism: the *Rig Veda*, *Yajur Veda*, *Sama Veda* and the *Atharva Veda*. A scholar, in this context, is therefore someone who has had instruction in one or more Vedas.

Similarly, greatness — the condition of being "exalted" — is identified with immersion in austere religious practices (tapas), or rigorous discipline such as the various yogas and meditation, which help focus one's mind and facilitate the understanding of one's true nature.

The "second," or supplementary, self referred to here is like a companion to oneself. What is the purpose of such a companion or shadow self? Yudhishthira suggests such a "double" watches over you and by controlling your mind, speech and behavior makes sure you stay in focus.

In the first three verses of Chapter 16 of the *Bhagavad Gita*, Lord Krishna conveys the prerequisite values necessary for realizing the divine state in straightforward and human terms:

> "Fearlessness, purity of heart, steadfastness in the pursuit of knowledge and yoga, alms-giving, control of the senses, sacrifice, the study of scriptures, austerity and straightforwardness.

> "Non-violence, truth, absence of anger, renunciation, peacefulness, absence of crookedness, compassion towards beings, non-covetousness, gentleness, modesty, absence of fickleness.
>
> "Vigor, forgiveness, fortitude, purity, absence of hatred, absence of pride, — these belong to the one born to the divine state, O Arjuna."

Sri Krishna lists a total of 26 with abhayam, or fearlessness, as the commander of this army of divine qualities. The quality of fortitude is not just desirable but essential.

Swami Vivekananda too recognized strength of mind as the keystone of character when he declared:

> "Know that all sins can be summed up in that one word — weakness. Fearlessness leads to strength and manhood."

Fear breeds weakness, timidity dehumanizes us and "creates us into moral monsters with an exaggerated sense of right and wrong, quick to judge, slow to forgive, legal in ethics and lacking in compassion, rigid in demand and unyielding in understanding."

Finally, serving elders, apprenticeship to knowledge, and the experience that comes with age helps in developing humility and learning about life, thus leading to wisdom.

To sum up, scholarship, rigorous religious devotion, courage and humility are the key requirements for living a life of dharma on earth.

Asks the Yaksha:	***Yudhishthira replies:***
किं ब्राह्मणानां देवत्वं कश्च धर्म: सतामिव कश्चैषां मानुषो भाव: किमेषामसतामिव	स्वाध्याय एषां देवत्वं तप एषां सतामिव मरणं मानुषो भाव: परिवादोऽसतामिव
kiṁ brāhmaṇānāṁ devatvaṁ	*svādhyāya eṣāṁ devatvaṁ*
kaśca dharmaḥ satāmiva	*tapa eṣāṁ satāmiva*
kaścaiṣāṁ mānuṣo bhāvaḥ	*maraṇam mānuṣo bhāvaḥ*
kimeṣāmasatāmiva	*parivādo astāmiva*
What marks divinity in brahmins?	Vedic knowledge.
What laws of theirs do the good share?	Tapasya.
What is their human attribute?	Mortality.
What makes them resemble the unworthy?	Slander.

~

The Yaksha's questions now turn towards testing Yudhishthira's understanding of the defining qualities of the various groups in society. The brahmins, the creators of knowledge and its teachers are the first group that the Yaksha asks Yudhishthira about.

Yudhishthira answers that the essential requirement for a brahmin to be god-like, distinctive in other words, lies in the worth of his scholarship of the Vedas.

The four Vedas are the origins of the Hindu thought. The Vedas stress the need to acquire two types of virtues: wisdom and courage. These are to be acquired through prayer and practice. Vedic prayers include prayers for intellectual power, efficiency, vigor, skill, strength and spiritual power. A perfect social organization, according to the Vedas, resulted from a balance between a philosophical and a social outlook. The Vedas urge human beings to search for truth rather than settle with beliefs. Truth according to the Vedas is the essence of divinity.

Tapasya (intense focus and immersion in austere practices) is an essential characteristic of brahmins. Anyone dedicated to such a working cause resembles brahmins in this quality.

Brahmins may seem god-like when involved in specialized Vedic rituals, practice and in their scholarship but they are, after all, human beings points out Yudhishthira as their mortality attests.

Brahmins can degrade from their special position by engaging in slander.

Yudhishthira is firm in holding that brahminhood is a standard — not a hereditary social position as is widely misunderstood — that distinguishes them from others. It requires very special devotion and hard work to acquire and maintain that quality. As stated in a later riddle, acquisition of that quality hinges on one and only one factor, namely one's character.

Asks the Yaksha:

किं क्षत्रियाणां देवत्वं
कश्च धर्म: सतामिव
कश्चैषां मानुषो भाव:
किमेषामसतामिव

kiṁ kṣatriyāṇāṁ devatvaṁ
kaśca dharmaḥ satāmiva
kaścaiṣāṁ mānuṣo bhāvaḥ
kimeṣāmasatāmiva

Yudhishthira replies:

इश्वस्त्रमेषां देवत्वं
यज्न एषां सतामिव
भयं वै मानुषो भाव:
परित्यागोऽसतामिव

iśvastrameṣām devatvaṁ
yajña eṣāṁ satāmiva
bhayaṁ vai mānuṣo bhāvaḥ
parityāgo' satāmiva

What marks divinity in the kshatriyas?	Skill in arms.
What practice do they (the kshatriyas) share with the good?	Yajnas.
What is their human attribute?	Fear.
When do they resemble the unworthy?	Abandoning the distressed.

~

Lest we suppose that devatvam (divinity or noble standard) was somehow reserved only for brahmins, this part of the dialogue makes it clear that others can also attain the same status. Only, the requirements are not the same as can be seen by comparising this and the previous set of answers. A person may choose whatever avocation that suits her or his personality and skills and seek perfection.

Thus, while the study of the Vedas was used as a yardstick to determine the potential of devatvam — a noble ("god-like") standard of goodness or excellence that can lead to moksha or salvation — for brahmins, the equivalent requirement for kshatriyas is their courage and skill in arms. What is worthwhile to note here is that *moksha* is not limited to any one group of people. This shloka clearly states how kshatriyas can attain the same status.

Yajna, sacrifice is inherent in a kshatriya's life. A kshatriya will not hesitate to give his life to protect and defend his country. The pious and the good practicing an elaborate fire ritual of yajna (homas) offering sacrifices to Agni resemble kshatriyas in this.

Death was the feature that makes one recognize that the brahmins too are mortal but death is an attribute a kshatriya welcomes in the course of the performance of his duty. Thus, the god-like kshatriya becomes a mere mortal when he exhibits the natural human characteristic of fear. It is fear that highlights the humanness of a kshatriya — for to be fearless is their ideal.

Since the essence of a kshatriya's dharma is protecting the society, abandonment of the distressed degrades a kshatriya.

Asks the Yaksha:	***Yudhishthira replies:***
किमेकं यज्ञियं साम किमेकं यज्ञियं यजुः का चैषां वृणुते यज्ञं कां यज्ञो नातिवर्तते	प्राणो वै यज्ञियं साम मनो वै यज्ञियं यजुः ऋगेका वृणुते यज्ञं तां यज्ञो नातिवर्तते
kimekaṁ yajñiyaṁ sāma *kimekaṁ yajñiyam yajuḥ* *kā caiṣāṁ vṛṇute yajñam* *kāṁ yajño nātivartate*	*prāṇo vai yajñiyaṁ sāma* *mano vai yajñiyam yajuḥ* *ṛgekā vṛṇute yajñaṁ* *tāṁ yajño nātivartate*
What makes the chant of a yajna?	Prāna.
What makes the yaju (sacrifice) of a yajna?	Mind.
What makes the refuge of a yajna?	*Rig Veda.*
Without what is there no yajna?	*Rig Veda.*

~

The primary goal of Hindus is moksha — release from the cycle of births and deaths. Yajnas serve as a mechanism to surrender and offer ourselves in a ritual to reach that goal. This self-sacrifice is that of the mind totally focused on the Supreme Being and completely immersed in worship.

Yajna is an ancient Vedic ritual of sacrifice undertaken to propitiate gods and goddesses. It remains popular in Hindu worship practice to this day. The chosen medium to reach the heavens where the gods reside is Agni, the fire god. Elaborate and precise rules are prescribed to build fire altars. In addition, the number of priests participating, mantras appropriate to the deity whose grace is being sought, and sacrifices to be made were all specified long ago. In established temples, a common sight is an attentive assembly of devotees enjoying the sight as fire in the agni kunda consumes incense, ghee, grains, coconut, new sarees and blouse pieces, and other offerings. A familiar refrain is the concluding declaration, *idam namama* ("this is not mine") at the end of each offering, acknowledging the Hindu belief that everything we have is not ours but belongs really to the deities.

The essential features of a yajna include priests knowledgeable in chants rendered with precise intonation and cadence, assembling offerings by types and in a systematic sequence, with a concluding set of prayers for the welfare of the families and the community. The fragrance that rises with the offerings is understood as pleasing to the assembly and to the gods.

A careful study of Yudhishthira 's answers suggests that the type of yajna implied here, while similar, is not a physical yajna. This inner yajna that Yudhishthira is talking about refers to the self within trying to connect with the Supreme Self. The process is all inside one's body and mind. The chant here is the very life force within — the prāna, the rhythmic breathing that sustains us.

And the yaju, the sacrifice? The very mind, whose surrender to the Lord is the sacrifice. Total immersion in the chanting of hymns, with or without a fire altar, leads to a meditative state which serves as a sanctuary to the seeker without which there is no yajna.

Asks the Yaksha:	***Yudhishthira replies:***
किं स्विदापततां श्रेष्ठं किं स्विन्निपततां वरम् किं स्वित्प्रतिष्ठमानानां किं स्वित्प्रवदतां वरम्	वर्षमापततां श्रेष्ठं बीजं निपततां वरम् गाव: प्रतिष्ठमानानां पुत्र: प्रवदतां वरम्
kiṁ svidāpatatāṁ śreṣṭaṁ *kiṁ svinnipatatāṁ varam* *kiṁ svitpratiṣṭhamānānāṁ* *kiṁ svitpravadatāṁ varam*	*varṣam* *bījaṁ* *gāvaḥ* *putraḥ*
What remains most beneficial even when it's falling?	Rain.
What remains most beneficial even when it's thrown down?	Seeds.
What is most sought by property seekers?	Cattle.
What is most desirable for those seeking progeny?	Sons.

~

To fully understand these questions and their answers we need to travel back in time thousands of years to Dwapara Yuga and appreciate the predominantly rural and agrarian society and culture then prevalent. Rain, quality seeds and cattle were especially important for the welfare of ancient societies and indeed continue to be desired for successful farming in any age. The desirability of sons needs to be viewed in the context of hard manual labor required in the fields to grow, harvest, store and market food products without machinery, as well as the future of a family. Sons remained within the traditional joint family system while daughters were married into other families.

Yugas: The Cycles of Time

Time, according to ancient Hindus is cyclical, not linear. Thus, there are no absolute beginnings and endings; time is simply a continuum. Hindus define periods of time that are cyclical in nature. Each cycle contains four sub-periods known as yugas (Krita or Satya Yuga, Treta Yuga, Dwapara Yuga and Kali Yuga). As one age passes into next, human values gradually decline and lead to dissolution before another period starts. Then the cycle repeats all over again.

Because of the cyclical nature of time, Hindus believe their religion is eternal and is properly called *Sanatana Dharma,* that is, Eternal Laws. Creation is without beginning or end, and there was no time when Brahman was not. In fact, time exists in Brahman.

Asks the Yaksha:

इन्द्रियार्थाननुभवन् बुद्धिमाल्लोकपूजितः
सम्मतः सर्वभूतानां उच्छ्वसन्को न जीवति

indriyārthānanubhavan buddhi māllokapūjitaḥ
sammataḥ sarvabhūtānāṁ ucchvasanko na jīvati

Is there a person who enjoys all pleasures of the senses, who is intelligent, is respected by all creatures and worshipped by the world, who breathes and yet is not alive?

Yudhishthira replies:

देवतातिथिभृत्यानां पितृणां आत्मनश्च यः
न नीर्वपति पञ्चानाम् उच्छ्वसन्न स जीवति

devatātithibṛtyānāṁ pitṛṇāṁ ātmanaśca yaḥ
na nirvapati pañcānām ucchvasan na sa jīvati

The person who fails to satisfy gods, guests, servants, *pitṛs* and his *ātman* may breathe but is not alive.

~

This dialogue underscores the standard by which a person can be deemed to be fully alive. To be alive in the world means to fulfill certain duties, discharge certain obligations; in other words, to be established in one's dharma. The reference to *pitṛs* (forefathers) emphasizes the Hindu reverence for the ancestral past. The reference to gods, guests and servants explains what must be given in return for the grace, pleasure, and respect received. The final requirement is self-respect. All these are to be viewed as components of a society that an individual must relate to. Yudhishthira stresses this relationship as the essential requirement to qualify a person as a human being.

In essence, what is being underscored is that we should recognize and fulfill our responsibilities to society.

In addition, the duties to oneself are equally important and these include a constant effort to gain knowledge of one's true nature.

Those who don't do so aren't truly alive, declares Yudhishthira.

Asks the Yaksha:	***Yudhishthira replies:***
किं स्विद्गुरुतरं भूमेः किं स्विदुच्चतरं च खात् किं स्विद्च्छीघ्रतरं वायोः किं स्विद्बहुतरं तृणाम्	माता गुरुतरा भूमेः खात्पितोच्चरस्तथा मनः शीघ्रतरं वाता चिन्ता बहुतरी तृणाम्
kiṁ svidgurutaraṁ bhūmeḥ *kiṁ sviduccataraṁ ca khāt* *kiṁ svid cchīghrataraṁ vāyoḥ* *kiṁ svidbahutaraṁ tṛṇām*	*mātā gurutarā bhūmeḥ* *khātpitoccatarastathā* *manaḥśīghrataram vātā* *cintā bahutarī tṛṇām*
What is weightier than earth?	Mother.
What is taller than the sky?	Father.
What is faster than the wind?	Mind.
What is more numerous than grass?	Thoughts.

~

The Yaksha now probes Yudhishthira's values and thinking.

Hindus call the earth Bhūmi Mātā — Mother Earth, and worship her as a mother. What, then, can be more important than earth? The mother who gives birth to us is more important, avers Yudhishthira. One's mother is verily god.

Similarly, Yudhishthira holds one's father to be of greater importance than even the sky. For us humans our parents who gave us life in this world are like gods, the highest, the most important beings. This is resonant with the Upanishadic pronoucement *"Mātṛ devo bhava, pitṛ devo bhava"* — May your mother and father be like gods to you.

In but an instant, one's mind can travel anywhere, everywhere — and back again. Which is why Yudhishthira says that mind is faster than the wind.

What can be more numerous than grass? Thoughts! Waves and waves of thoughts arise in our minds constantly, and move on. There is no end to this process. They grow and grow and continue to grow in newer and newer layers and waves — far more numerous than grass.

In these responses, Yudhishthira underlines the reason and importance of respecting one's parents.

He also emphasizes the importance of keeping our mind under control, watching over our thoughts, weeding out unnecessary worries, and not giving them so much importance.

Asks the Yaksha:	***Yudhishthira replies:***
किं स्वित्सुप्तं न निमिषति किं स्विज्जातं न चोपति कस्य स्विद्धृदयं नास्ति किं स्विद्वेगेन वर्धते	मत्स्यः सुप्तो न निमिषत्यण्डं जातं न चोपति अश्मनो हृदयं नास्ति नदी वेगेन वर्धते
kiṁ svit suptaṁ na nimiṣati *kiṁ svijjātaṁ na copati* *kasya sviddhṛdayaṁ nāsti* *kiṁ svidvegena vardhate*	*matsyaḥ supto na nimiṣatyaṇḍaṁ jātaṁ na copati* *aśmano hṛdayaṁ nāsti nadī vegena vardhate*
What sleeps with its eyes open?	A fish.
What remains still even after birth?	An egg.
What has no heart?	A stone.
What swells quickly by itself?	A river.

~

Yudhishthira's sutra-like crisp answers appear obvious at the physical level but in India's Vedic and epic literature, the sutras contain in their coils, multiple layers of meaning.

Thus, for example, the ātman, residing in the body, is awake and alert even when the body is in a state of dream or deep sleep. A similar interpretation is offered for having "no heart" in that while the various organs including the heart are a part of the body, but not the ātman, and neither does the ātman distinguish between pleasure and pain. Thus, the learned (jnāni) disassociate themselves from the body and cultivate indifference towards its pleasure and pain. The "swelling" of the river is interpreted to mean the increasing levels of consciousness of the seeker in a deep meditative state.

Asks the Yaksha:	***Yudhishthira replies:***
किं स्वित्प्रवसतो मित्रं किं स्विन्मित्रं गृहे सतः आतुरस्य च किं मित्रं किं स्विन्मित्रं मरिष्यतः	सार्थः प्रवसतो मित्रं भार्या मित्रं गृहे सतः आतुरस्य भिषङ्मित्रं दानं मित्रं मरिष्यतः
kiṁsvit pravasato mitraṁ *kiṁ svinmitraṁ gṛhe sataḥ* *aturasya ca kiṁ mitraṁ* *kiṁ svinmitraṁ mariṣyataḥ*	*sārthaḥ pravasato mitraṁ* *bharyāmitraṁ gṛhesataḥ* *aturasya bhiṣaṅmitraṁ* *dānam mitraṁ mariṣyataḥ*
Who is the traveler's friend?	A companion.
Who is the householder's friend?	A spouse.
Who is the friend of the sick?	A doctor.
Who is the friend of the dying?	His charity.

~

This group of questions and answers stresses the need for and the role of friends, and the importance for everyone to be involved with others in a mutual, healthy, giving and receiving of support. The first three friendships referred to in these questions involve other people but the last category, the friend at the end of one's life, is one's own lifetime of charitable giving.

Yudhishthira's answers here are straightforward and clear. For, a traveler's best friend is indeed a companion traveler.

A householder's true friend is his wife. In a ritual known as *sapta padi,* a Hindu man takes the woman he is marrying by the hand at the wedding ceremony and walks seven steps with her around the fire as both pledge their eternal friendship to each other.

The man says: "With these seven steps you have become my life's companion. We are both friends. I shall never fail to be your friend. May you also never fail to be my friend . . . ."

This is the understanding, the promise, the commitment that binds a Hindu couple. Which is why his spouse is considered the householder's best friend.

For a sick person, clearly the most desirable friend is a doctor.

For the dying, the charity done during his or her lifetime serves as a true friend by providing a sense of fulfillment and preparation for the life to come. This idea is reinforced in Verse 17 of the *Ishopanishad* — Mind! Remember! Remember thy deeds!

Asks the Yaksha:

कोऽतिथिः सर्वभूतानां
किंस्विद्धर्मं सनातनम्
अमृतं किम्स्विद्राजेन्द्र
किंस्वित्सर्वमिदं जगत्

ko'tithiḥ sarva bhūtānāṁ
kiṁ sviddharmaṁ sanātanam
amṛtaṁ kiṁ svidrājendra
kiṁ svitsarvamidaṁ jagat

Who is the guest of all creatures?
What is the eternal Dharma?
What is amrita?
What is this entire universe?

Yudhishthira replies:

अतिथिः सर्वभूतानामग्निः
सनातनोमृतो धर्मो
सोमो गवामृतम्
वायुः सर्वमिदं जगत्

atithiḥ sarvabhutānamagniḥ
sanātanomṛto dharmo
somo gavāmṛtam
vayuḥ sarvamidaṁ jagat

Agni.
Amrita.
Cow's milk.
Air.

~

As noted earlier, the most revered Vedic god Agni plays an important role in rituals and is treated as the medium to convey prayers offered during *homas* (fire ceremonies). It also represents the physical fire of hunger which is a constant "guest" for all living beings.

Yudhishthira avers that Agni, fire, is the guest residing in every living being. The fire here is the fire within — inside the belly — waiting to be served and fed!

In this shloka, there is also a beautiful play on the word *amrita,* which means both the nectar of immortality and food of the gods. In translating *gavāmṛtam* the poet uses nectar as equivalent to cow's milk so essential for growth of humans. When it relates to dharma, the same word is interpreted as that which has no death, (*amrita*) namely eternal! Further, this entire universe is air.

Asks the Yaksha:	***Yudhishthira replies:***
किं स्विदेको विचरते जातः को जायते पुनः किं स्वित् हिमस्य भैषज्यं किं स्विदावपनं महत्	सूर्य एको विचरते चन्द्रमा जायते पुनः अग्निर्हिमस्य भैषज्यं भूमिरावपनं महत्
kiṁ svideko vicaraté	*sūrya eko vicaraté*
jātaḥ ko jāyate punaḥ	*candramā jāyate punaḥ*
kiṁ svit himasya bhaiṣajyaṁ	*agnirhimasya bhaiṣajyaṁ*
kiṁ svidāvapanaṁ mahat	*bhūmirāvapanaṁ mahat*
What moves about alone?	The sun.
Who, once born, is born again?	The moon.
What is the remedy against cold?	Fire (Agni).
Which is the largest vessel?	Earth.

~

Again, we need to understand this set of questions and Yudhishthira's answers at two levels.

At the basic physical level, the sun is alone as it "travels" because for people on earth its brilliance masks the millions of other luminous bodies that become visible at night.

Similarly, the moon goes through visible phases, waxing and waning, to re-emerge anew after each dark New Moon day to reach its full potential on the Full Moon day. Heat counters cold. The earth is the sacred space where one sows seed (makes offerings).

At another level, the individual self (ātman) can be seen as the one that travels the cycle of births and deaths and thus always "moves alone." At this microcosmic level, upon the death of a body, the soul, depending on its accumulated karma, finds itself in another new-born body and, through its radiance, is born the mind of the baby. This is equated to the moon which is described as being "born again and again" in the well-known blessing mantra, beginning with "*navo navo bhavati.*"*

In this context, Agni is the fire of self-knowledge that destroys ignorance (fog) about one's true nature.

* Srinivasan, A.V., *The Vedic Wedding: Origins, Tradition and Practice*, p. 144.

Asks the Yaksha:	***Yudhishthira replies:***
किंस्विदेकपदं धर्म्यं किंस्विदेकपदं यशः किंस्विदेकपदं स्वर्ग्यं किंस्विदेकपदं सुखं	दाक्ष्यमेकपदम् धर्म्यं दानमेकपदं यशः सत्यमेकपदं स्वर्ग्यं शीलमेकपदं सुखं
kiṁ svidekapadaṁ dharmyaṁ *kiṁ svidekapadaṁ yaśaḥ* *kiṁ svidekapadaṁ svargyaṁ* *kiṁ svidekapadaṁ sukhaṁ*	*dākṣyamekapadam dharmyaṁ* *danamekapadaṁ yaśaḥ* *satyamekapadaṁ svargyaṁ* *śīlamekapadaṁ sukhaṁ*
What in one word is dharma?	Skill.
What in one word is fame?	Charity.
What in one word is heaven?	Truth.
What in one word is happiness?	Character.

~

Yudhishthira's one-word answers here are a guide to the qualities needed to develop skills relevant to one's own dharma, practice of which is believed to lead to fame, heaven and happiness.

The essence of one's dharma lies in possessing a certain ability or skill to perform duties pertinent to the function associated with that dharma. For example, *kshatriya* dharma requires acquisition and development of skills in warfare. It may also refer to ritual skill, skill to acquire will power and strength of a spiritual nature.

Giving, sharing, offering one's money, time and ideas so that someone else may benefit, all lead to our own as well as society's well-being — and also lead to fame.

The Hindu interpretation of heaven is that it is the abode of truth.

The true essence of happiness is steadfast character.

Asks the Yaksha:	***Yudhishthira replies:***
किं स्विदात्मा मनुष्यस्य किं स्विद्दैवकृतः सखा उपजीवनं किं स्विदस्य किं स्विदस्य परायणं	पुत्र आत्मा मनुष्यस्य भार्या दैवकृतः सखा उपजीवनंच पर्जन्यो दानमस्य परायणं
kiṁ svidātmā manuṣyasya *kiṁ sviddaivakṛtaḥ sakhā* *upajīvanaṁ kiṁ svidasya* *kiṁ svidasya parāyaṇaṁ*	*putra ātmā manuṣyasya* *bhāryā daivakṛtaḥ sakhā* *upajīvanaṁca parjanyo* *dānamasya parāyaṇaṁ*
What is a man's self?	His progeny.
Who is his God-given friend?	His spouse.
What supports his life?	Rain.
What is the principal goal?	Charity.

~

The dialogue between the Yaksha and Yudhishthira now turns to areas that are immediate to a person: children, spouse, the element essential to sustain life, community, and the concept of sharing.

Thus, says Yudhishthira, that a man's progeny represents the physical reflection and extension of his own self.

One's wife is one's best friend, as discussed in an earlier question.

Man's most basic physical need for food can be met only by adequate rainfall for crops.

And charity implies giving and sharing, the foundation for community life.

Asks the Yaksha:	***Yudhishthira replies:***
धन्यानां उत्तरं किं स्विद् धनानां स्यात्किं उत्तमं लाभानांउत्तमं किंस्यात् सुखानां स्यात्किमुत्तमं	धन्यानां उत्तरं दाक्ष्यं धनानामुत्तरं शृतं लाभानां श्रेय आरोग्यं सुखानां तुष्टिरुत्तमं
dhanyānāṁ uttaraṁ kiṁ svid	*dākṣyaṁ*
dhanānāṁ syāt kiṁ uttamaṁ	*śrutaṁ*
labhānāṁuttamaṁ kiṁ syāt	*ārogyaṁ*
sukhānām syāt kiṁ uttamaṁ	*tuṣṭi*
Which treasure is the best?	Skill.
Which wealth is the best?	Education.
What is the greatest gain?	Health.
And the greatest happiness?	Contentment.

~

Time and again Hindu philosophy emphasizes skill and learning as essential aspects for a successful life. Similarly, good health of mind and body is declared the best of gains and contentment the greatest happiness.

Therefore one may conclude the following:

We should develop skills in areas which interest us most and continue to have those skills in order to excel.

The emphasis in our lives should be on acquiring knowledge, especially spiritual knowledge.

A person who is not contented, and is a slave to greed, is a slave to everyone. On the other hand, a person who can en-slave desire rules the world.

These questions and answers provide a practical guide to mental, social and physical well-being.

Asks the Yaksha	***Yudhishthira replies:***
कश्च धर्मः परो लोके कश्च धर्मः सदाफलः किं नियम्य न शोचंति कैश्च संधिर्न जीर्यते	अनृशमस्यं परोधर्मः त्रयीधर्मः सदाफलः मनोयम्य न शोचंति संधिः सद्भिर्नजीर्यते
kaśca dharmaḥ paroloke	*anṛśamasyaṁ parodharmaḥ*
kaśca dharmaḥ sadāphalaḥ	*trayīdharmaḥ sadāphalaḥ*
kiṁ niyamya naśocaṁti	*manoyamya naśocaṁti*
kaishca sandhirna jīryate	*sandhiḥ sadbhirnajīryate*
What is the supreme dharma in the world?	Non-maliciousness.
Which dharma always bears fruit?	Vedic dharma.
By restraining what is one free from grief?	Mind.
Between whom does a bond not wither?	Good people.

~

Yudhishthira's answers here may serve as guidelines for both self development and spiritual growth.

Refraining from harming others — non-violence or ahimsa — is the greatest dharma. This is the principle that Mahatma Gandhi also made the very core of his life.

Vedic dharma emphasizes acquiring a unique combination of spiritual brilliance (brahma teja) and physical prowess (kshatra veerya) through learning and training.

Lack of restraint over one's own mind may lead to wrong thoughts — and so to wrong actions, unhappiness and grief. Which is why Yudhishthira highlights restraint over one's mind as the single most important factor in overcoming grief and being happy. Krishna teaches Arjuna the same lesson in the *Bhagavad Gita*.

As the bond between good people rests on their inherent goodness, it leads to enduring bonds. Higher forms of friendship, according to Mortimer Adler,* citing Aristotle, ".... must be based on virtue, on a good moral character. Only in that way can it last. Further, it must develop slowly, since it presupposes familiarity, knowledge, and — eventually — mutual trust." Such friendship is never wasted.

---

* *Great Ideas from the Great Books,* Washington Square Press, 1963, p. 261.

Asks the Yaksha:	***Yudhishthira replies:***
किं नु हित्वा प्रियो भवति किं नु हित्वा न शोचति किं नु हित्वार्थवान् भवति किं नु हित्वा सुखी भवेत्	मानं हित्वा प्रियो भवति क्रोधं हित्वा न शोचति कामं हित्वार्थवान् भवति लोभं हित्वा सुखी भवेत्
kiṁ nu hitvā priyo bhavati *kiṁ nu hitvā na śocati* *kiṁ nu hitvārthavān bhavati* *kiṁ nu hitvā sukhī bhavet*	*mānaṁ hitvā priyo bhavati* *krodhaṁ hitvā na śocati* *kāmaṁ hitvārthavān bhavati* *lobhaṁ hitvā sukhī bhavet*
By renouncing what does one become lovable?	Pride.
By renouncing what is one free of sorrow?	Anger.
By renouncing what does one become wealthy?	Desire.
By renouncing what does one become happy?	Greed.

~

The dialogue continues to delineate qualities that encourage personal and spiritual growth.

Yaksha's questions focus on issues important to all of us, for everyone wants to be loved, to be free of sorrow, to be happy and prosperous.

Yudhishthira's answers involve controlling and training the mind in such a way that we can gradually get rid of the enemies, namely these qualities which take us off-course, within us: pride, anger, desire and greed.

When one understands the transient nature of happiness that fulfillment of desire brings, there is little need for an excess of material possessions. One's sense of well-being, the real meaning of wealth, then increases of its own. Wealth is viewed here in the context of what one may have in relation to one's desire.

Asks the Yaksha:

किमर्थं ब्राह्मणे दानं
किमर्थं नटनर्तके
किमर्थं चैव भृत्येषु
किमर्थं चैव राजसु

kimarthaṁ brāhmaṇe dānaṁ
kimarthaṁ naṭanartake
kimarthaṁ caiva bhṛtyeṣu
kimarthaṁ caiva rājasu

Why is one charitable to brahmins?
Why does one support actors, dancers?
Why does one give to those who serve us?
Why does one pay (taxes) to kings?

Yudhishthira replies:

धर्मार्थं ब्राह्मणे दानं
यशोर्थं नट नर्तके
भृत्येषु भरणार्थं
भयार्थंचैव राजसु

dharmārthaṁ brahmaṇe dānaṁ
yaśorthaṁ naṭanartake
bhṛtyeṣu bharaṇārthaṁ
bhayārthaṁcaiva rājasu

As dharma.
To gain renown.
For their livelihood.
Out of fear.

~

The dialogue moves on the relationship between a giver and recipient, and the benefits both may gain. The act of giving and receiving underlines social relationships and the need for mutual, adequate support and respect in a society.

The first question here pertains to giving and receiving. While discussing giving to a brahmin, it is essential to recall the definition of a brahmin. The giving in the context of this question is to a person who by his attainment in spiritual matters is a repository of true wisdom essential to a successful society. In addition, he or she possesses that singular feature that distinguishes the brahmin aspect, namely strength of character. The latter should be evident in the intended recipients; then and only then, are they fit to receive. That, of course, describes the receiver.

But what about the giver? Why should one give to brahmins? According to Yudhishthira, one gives to brahmins for the sake of dharma, that is, as a special duty. It is in this special context that the giving to brahmins is to be understood. In the process the giver receives the benefit of the spiritual strength of the receiver and the brahmin's knowledge through teaching.

The support of artists, compensation to those who serve, and the payment of taxes are all considered to be important duties of a conscientious citizen. In supporting artists and performers, culture is preserved beyond the performance and the art form: the fame and generosity of the donor are also noted. The last three sets of questions and answers are amazingly clear and immediate in statement and intent, requiring little elucidation.

Asks the Yaksha:	***Yudhishthira replies:***
केन स्विदावृतो लोकः केन स्विन्न प्रकाशते केन त्यजति मित्राणि केन स्वर्गं न गच्छति	अज्नानेनावृतो लोकस् तमसा न प्रकाशते लोभात्त्यजति मित्राणि सङ्गात्स्वर्गं न गच्छति
kenasvidāvṛto lokaḥ *kenasvinnaprakāśate* *kena tyajati mitrāṇi* *kena svargaṁ na gacchati*	*ajnānenāvṛto lokas* *tamasā naprakāśate* *lobhāttyajati mitṛāṇi* *saṅgāt svargaṁ na gacchati*
What engulfs the world?	Ignorance.
What prevents the world from illumination?	Spiritual darkness.
Why does one forsake friends?	Greed.
What limits one's attainment of heaven?	Attachment.

~

Ignorance of one's true nature is the spiritual darkness that engulfs the world, replies Yudhishthira in response to Yaksha's query. This ignorance is universal as Swami Vivekananda said "— ignorance is the great mother of all misery and the fundamental ignorance is to think that the Infinite weeps and cries, that it is finite. This is the basis of all ignorance — that we, the immortal, the ever pure, the perfect spirit think we are little minds, we are little bodies."*

That is the reason for the prayer *"Tamaso mā jyotir gamaya."* The prayer is a plea to the Lord to lead us from darkness to light (*Brihadaranyaka Upanishad*).

An overpowering desire for material possessions and power and attachment to the fruits of action is the weakness which prevents true relationships and true happiness. This theme recurs in the *Bhagavad Gita,* where Krishna instructs Arjuna in the essence of karma yoga.

Ignorance, greed, desire, attachment are chains that bind us to think of ourselves as ever-limited beings and prevent us both from understanding our true nature of Brahman and reaching our spiritual goals.

---

* *Vivekananda, The Yogas and Other Works,* Swami Nikhilandanda, Ramakrishna-Vivekananda Center, New York, 1953, p. 215.

Asks the Yaksha:	***Yudhishthira replies:***
मृतः कथं स्यात्पुरुषः कथं राष्ट्रं मृतं भवेत् श्राद्धं मृतं कथं वा स्यात्कथं यज्ञो मृतोभवेत्	मृतो दरिद्रः पुरुषः मृतं राष्ट्रमराजकं मृतमश्रोत्रियं श्राद्धं मृतो यज्ञस्त्वदक्षिणः
mṛtaḥ kathaṁ syātpuruṣaḥ *kathaṁ rāṣṭraṁṛtaṁ bhavet* *śrāddhaṁ mṛtaṁ kathaṁ vā* *syātkathaṁ yajno mṛtobhavet*	*daridraḥ puruṣaḥ* *rāṣṭramarājakaṁ* *aśrotriyaṁ* *adakṣiṇaḥ*
What makes a man dead?	(When) he is poor.
What makes a nation dead?	(When) it's without a ruler.
What makes a shrāddha dead?	(When) led by the ignorant.
What makes a yajnā dead?	(When) no gift is offered.

~

These four questions of the Yaksha relate to conditions of weakness in the individual and society: poverty, political vacuum, ignorant priests, shirking of commitments, all of which are to be avoided.

The ancients warn us of the danger of falling into the pit of abject poverty — it is akin to being dead while alive. The dead, of course, have no wealth except the baggage of their own karma.

Historically, nations have often fallen or dwindled away at the death of a great ruler. Which is why modern states permit as little delay as possible between changes in government. "The King is dead; long live the King!" the familiar refrain of England rings true in this context.

Also, without a good ruler a country is essentially dead.

Shrāddha is any work performed with *shraddha* (faith). One must be careful in selecting a knowledgeable person to lead in all dharmic work.

Similarly, the performance of a yajna requires a knowledgeable person for its conduct and guidance and that requires considerable effort. Therefore appropriate fees — dakshina — must be offered to the conducting priest in order to perform a successful yajna. The exchange, i.e. assistance, received in the proper conduct of a yajna and the gift accepted in return should be viewed as a necessary spiritual equation.

Asks the Yaksha:	***Yudhishthira replies:***
का दिक्किमुदकं प्रोक्तं किमन्नं किं च वै विशम् श्राद्धस्य कालमाख्याहि	सन्तो दिग्जलमाकाशं गौरान्नं प्रार्थना विशम् श्राद्धस्य ब्राह्मणः कालः
kā dikkimudakaṁ proktaṁ *kimannaṁ kiṁ ca vai viśam* *shrāddhasya kālamākhyāhi*	*santo digjalamākāśaṁ* *gaurānnaṁ prārthanā viśam* *śrāddhasya brāhmaṇaḥ kālaḥ*
What is the direction (one should take)?	The way of the good.
What are water, food and poison?	Sky; cow products; begging.
What is the right time for a shrāddha?	A learned brahmin's time.

~

Whom does one follow in life? Whom should we look up to? Whom can one trust, now asks the Yakshas?

Yudhishthira says that the example of good people is the path one needs to take. This question comes up again in another set of questions with a more specific wording (What is the path?).

Virtuous (dhārmic) and knowledgeable people are the sources of direction for most people striving to lead a meaningful life — a refrain heard and seen throughout Vedic philosophy!

The sky is the source where clouds gather and rain showers develop, and is here equated to the essential commodity, water. Cow's milk and ghee were considered by pastoral ancient Aryans as essential for human health and growth. Ghee is also offered to Agni in homas (fire rituals), and thus its additional importance.

It is intriguing to note the ancients' view of poverty and begging as poison! A way of life that diminished self respect was obviously to be avoided.

The right time for performing a shrāddha is when a learned brahmin is available. It is interesting to note from Yudhishthira's answer that the most important consideration is not any particular auspicious time or day but the availability of proper guidance from a knowledgeable person.

Asks the Yaksha:	***Yudhishthira replies:***
तपः किं लक्षणं प्रोक्तं को दमश्च प्रकीर्तितः क्षमा च का परा प्रोक्ता का च ह्रीः परिकीर्तिता	तपः स्वधर्मवर्तित्वं मनसो दमनं दमः क्षमा द्वन्द्व सहिष्णुत्वं ह्रीरकार्यनिवर्तनम्
tapaḥ kiṁ lakṣanaṁ proktaṁ	*tapaḥ svadharmavartitvaṁ*
ko damaśca prakīrtitaḥ	*manaso damanaṁ damaḥ*
kṣamā ca kā parā proktā	*kṣamā dvandva sahiṣṇutvaṁ*
kā ca hrīḥ parikīrtatā	*hrirakāryanivartanam*
What constitutes impeccability?	Following one's own dharma.
What is discipline?	Restraint of one's mind.
What is forbearance?	Tolerating opposites.
What constitutes a sense of shame?	Backing away from unacceptable behavior.

~

The dialogue here between the Yaksha and Yudhishthira covers several important dimensions of life.

Tapas, or tapasya, can here be understood as leading an impeccable life by rigorously following dharma on a daily basis even as we enjoy life in its fullness. It does not mean withdrawal or inaction, or punishment for crime or sins. Practicing one's own dharma, in accordance with one's background, education and training, in order to serve society without focusing on rewards or results, constitutes tapasya.

Discipline in daily life is traced for mental focus and restraing one's mind from going adrift in all directions.

Tolerating diverse points of view is emphasized a key for peaceful living in a diverse society and a diverse world.

And an in-built sense of propriety and a sense of shame prevents one from unethical and unacceptable behavior.

Asks the Yaksha:	***Yudhishthira replies:***
किं ज्नानं प्रोच्यते राजन् कः शमश्च प्रकीर्तितः दया च का परा प्रोक्ता किं चार्जवं उदाहृतं	ज्नानं तत्वार्थ संबोधः शमश्चित्त प्रशांतता दया सर्व सुखैष्वितं आर्जवं समचित्तता
kiṁ jnānaṁ procyate rājan	*jnānaṁ tatvārtha sambodhaḥ*
kaḥ śamaśca prakīrtitaḥ	*śamaścitta praśāntatā*
dayā ca kā parā proktā	*dayā sarva sukhaiṣvitaṁ*
kiṁ cārjavaṁ udāhṛtaṁ	*ārjavaṁ samacittatā*
What is knowledge?	Cognition of the true nature of things.
What is tranquility?	A serene mind.
What is the supreme compassion?	Wishing the happiness of all.
What is simplicity?	A poised mind.

~

Vedic Hindus believed that all knowledge, secular or spiritual, is present in the human mind. The mind is like a mine but it has a cover on it. The process of uncovering it, removing the veil of ignorance, is learning. Eastern thinkers prescribe the goal of man to be knowledge because they conclude that it is through knowledge (not opinions or beliefs) that one can be truly free.

Peace of mind, the true goal of everyone, and tranquility are the same, according to Yudhishthira.

To wish well for everyone is the supreme compassion. Vedic prayers always end with the wish: "*Sarve janā: sukhino bhavantu,*" meaning "May all people be happy."

And, to be intelligent is to be poised in all circumstances.

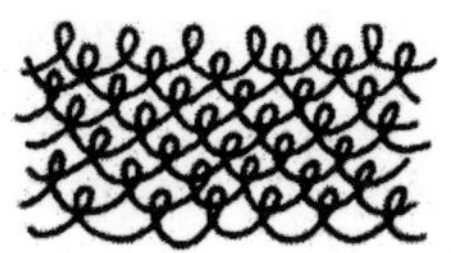

Asks the Yaksha:	***Yudhishthira replies:***
कः शत्रुर्दुर्जयः पुंसाम् कश्च व्याधिरनंतकः कीदृशश्च स्मृतः साधुर् असाधुः कीदृशः स्मृतः	क्रोधः सुदुर्जयः शत्रुर् लोभो व्याधिरनंतकः सर्व भूतहितः साधुर् असाधुर्निर्दय स्मृतः
kaḥ śatrurdurjayaḥ pumsām *kaśca vyādhiranantakaḥ* *kīdṛśaśca smṛtaḥ sādhur* *asādhuḥ kīdṛśaḥ smṛtaḥ*	*krodhaḥ sudurjayaḥ śatrur* *lobho vyādhiranantakaḥ* *sarva bhūtahitaḥ sādhur* *asādhurnirdaya smṛtaḥ*
Which enemy is nearly impossible to conquer?	Anger.
What is man's endless disease?	Greed.
Who is good?	One who seeks the good of all.
Who is not good?	One who lacks compassion.

~

Anger, asserts Yudhishthira, is a human being's great enemy: Anger clouds the mind's capacity to think clearly, and so on. And greed, potentially never-ending, of wanting more and more is truly a disease as it pulls a person away from happiness and peace of mind. They lead us to *adhārmic* conduct.

The true piety, cited here as the quality of good people, is love of one's fellow creatures, ranked above attachment to dogma or religious observances. Lacking compassion in one's interactions with other beings is dubbed as "not good."

Asks the Yaksha:	***Yudhishthira replies:***
कोमोहः प्रोच्यते राजन् कश्च मानः प्रकीर्तितः किमालस्यं च विज्ञेयम् कश्च शोकः प्रकीर्तितः	मोहो हि धर्ममूढत्वं मानस्त्वात्माभिमानता धर्मनिष्क्रियतालस्यं शोकस्त्व ज्ञानमुच्यते
komohaḥ procyate rājan *kaśca mānaḥ prakīrtitaḥ* *kimālasyaṁ ca vijñeyaṁ* *kaśca śokaḥ prakīrtitaḥ*	*moho hi dharmamūḍatvaṁ* *Manastvātmābhimānatā* *dharmaniṣkriyatālasyaṁ* *śokastvajñānamucyate*
What is delusion?	Inability to grasp the essentials of dharma.
What is pride?	An exaggerated sense of self-importance.
What is laziness?	Not acting dharmically.
What is grief?	Ignorance.

~

This set of questions and answers cautions the seeker not to ignore one's own dharma and not be self-conscious. It further condemns laziness and equates grief with ignorance of reality. Ancient Hindus stressed relentlessly the need to live within the framework of dharma, obtain knowledge of the self leading to humility and dynamic detached action.

Asks the Yaksha:

किं स्थैर्यमृशिभिः प्रोक्तं
किं च धैर्यमुदाहृतं
स्नानंच किं परं प्रोक्तं
दानं च किमि होच्यते

kiṁ sthairyamṛśibhiḥ proktaṁ
kiṁ ca dhairyamudāhṛtaṁ
snānaṁca kiṁ paraṁ proktaṁ
dānaṁ ca kimihocyate

What do the sages call steadfastness?
What is courage?
What is the supreme cleansing?
What is charity?

Yudhishthira replies:

स्वधर्मे स्थिरता स्थैर्यं
धैर्यमिंद्रिय निग्रहं
स्नानं मनोमल त्यागो
दानं वै भूतरक्षणं

svadharme sthiratā sthairyaṁ
dhairyamindriya nigrahaṁ
snānaṁ manomala tyāgo
dānaṁ vai bhūtarakṣaṇāṁ

Being rooted in one's own dharma.
Keeping one's senses in check.
Cleansing of the mind.
Protection of all creatures.

~

This dialogue here takes forward the ideas presented earlier in regard to personal qualities. The qualities of steadfastness and courage are given a new meaning. The importance of keeping the mind under control and of sticking to one's own values are stressed. Charity is extended to include all living things.

Dharma is now explained in a personal context as steadfastness to one's own way of life or chosen principles. This, in turn, requires purifying and controlling one's mind

The reference to protection of all creatures, namely maintaining an ecological balance by respecting nature rings so appropriate in this age considering the damage societies around the world have done to the environment and the associated impact to healthy living. Ancient Hindus recognized that it is the duty of human beings to sustain all living beings and protect the environment.

Asks the Yaksha:	***Yudhishthira replies:***
कः पंडितः पुमाज्ञ्नेयो नास्तिकः कश्च उच्यते को मूर्खः कश्च कामः स्यात्को मत्सर इति स्मृतः	धर्मज्ञ्नः पण्डितो ज्ञेयो नास्तिको मूर्ख उच्यते कामः संसारहेतुश्च हृत्तापो मत्सरः स्मृतः
kaḥ panditaḥ pumājñeyo *nāstikaḥ kaśca ucyate* *ko mūrkhaḥ kaśca kāmaḥ* *syātko matsara iti smṛtaḥ*	*dharmajnaḥ pandito jñeyo* *nāstiko mūrkha ucyate* *kāmaḥ samsārahetuśca* *hṛttāpo matsaraḥ smṛtaḥ*
Who qualifies to be called wise?	One who knows dharma.
Who is an atheist?	Said to be a fool.
Who is a fool?	One who is covetous.
What is desire?	The cause of rebirth.
What is jealousy?	Heartache.

~

Knowledge of dharma and its vast implications as the basis of self-knowledge are a Hindu's definition of a wise person, a pandit. The harsh comment on atheism needs to be read in context because Hinduism allows and respects individual's choice of reaching one's goal and that includes not believing! However, we must note that the Pandavas are nearing the end of their 12-years exile: a humiliating experience soon to be followed by a year of even more humiliation and embarrassment as they live incognito. An exemplar of an atheist, for the Pandavas, is their cousin Duryodhana whose policies and actions revolve around gaining material possessions, irrespective of the means employed. This prince has broken all the rules of dharma. Thus the obvious view about atheism!

Lust and jealousy are beyond the framework of dharma even while Hindu philosophy recognizes artha (materialism) and kama (sensory pleasures) as legitimate components of a good life.

Asks the Yaksha:	***Yudhishthira replies:***
कोऽअहंकार: इति प्रोक्ता कश्च दंभ: प्रकीर्तित: किं तद्दैवं परं प्रोक्तं किं तत्पैशुन्यमुच्यते	महाज्ञानमहंकारो दंभो धर्मध्वजोच्छ्रय: दैवं दानफलं प्रोक्तं पैशुन्यं परदूशणं
ko'ahaṁkāraḥ iti proktā	*mahājñānamahaṁkāro*
kaśca daṁbhaḥ prakīrtitaḥ	*daṁbho dharmadhvajocchṛayaḥ*
kiṁ taddaivaṁ paraṁ proktaṁ	*daivaṁ dānaphalaṁ proktaṁ*
kiṁ tatpaiśunyamucyate	*paiśunyaṁ paradūśaṇaṁ*
What is egoism?	Total ignorance of one's true nature.
What is hypocrisy?	Pretending to be dharmic.
What is divine?	Fruits of charity.
What is vice?	Slandering others.

~

Yudhishthira's answers here may appear paradoxical on the surface. For, often we come across egoistic persons — even among scholars and prominent people. But being full of one's own individuality is indeed a sign of ignorance of one's real nature: Brahman. Thus, the stronger this belief in one's own individuality, the greater the ignorance.

In the answers, note the clever connection between *daiva* (divine) and *dāna* (charity). It is *dana*, the charitable deed, that is divine, not the doer. One does one's duty and no reward is claimed and that, according to Yudhishthira is being divine!

Asks the Yaksha:

धर्मश्चार्थश्च कामश्च परस्पर विरोधिनः
एषां नित्य विरुद्धानां कथमेकत्र संगमः

dharmaścārthaśca kāmaśca paraspara virodhinaḥ
eṣām nitya viruddhānāṁ kathamekatra sangamaḥ

Dharma, artha and kāma conflict with each other.
How can these contraries be reconciled?

Yudhishthira replies:

यदा धर्मश्च भार्या च परस्परवशानुगौ
तदा धर्मार्थकामानां त्रयाणामपि संगमः

yadā dharmaśca bhāryāca paraspara vaśānugau
tadā dharmārtha kāmānāṁ trayāṇāmapi sangamaḥ

When dharma and one's spouse are in harmony,
dharma, artha and kāma are reconciled.

~

The special role and contribution of a wife described above is the basis for Hindus to refer to a wife as *dharmapatni*, i.e. wife-in-dharma.

Yaksha's question highlights that a householder has to live with conflicting requirements and therefore the need for the restraints of dharma on *artha* (statecraft, money, material world) and *kāma* (emotional attachments). The attainment of *mokṣa,* i.e. salvation, is the highest goal propounded by ancient Hindus but it does not preclude full participation in the affairs of society, raising a family, enjoying the good life, serving the community . . . all within that framework known as dharma.

Yudhishthira's reply underscores that in order to keep that balance, a man has to have a wife who is dharmic. It is the protection and support afforded by the wife, that torchlight, that spirit of cooperation and sacrifice, which gives a man a reasonable chance to meet the challenge of these seemingly conflicting goals.

Asks the Yaksha:

अक्षयो नरकः केन प्राप्यते भरतर्शभ
एतन्मे पृच्छतः प्रश्नं तच्छीघ्रं वक्तुमर्हसि

akṣayo narakaḥ kena prāpyate bharatarśabha
etanme pṛcchataḥ praśnaṁ tacchīghraṁ vaktumarhasi

How does one obtain permanent hell? Answer this question quickly!

Yudhishthira replies:

ब्राह्मणं स्वयमाहूय याचमानमकिन्चनं
पश्चान्नास्तीति यो ब्रूयात्सो क्षयं नरकं व्रजेत्

brāhmaṇaṁ svayamāhūya yācamānamakincanam
paścānnāstīti yo brūyātsokṣayaṁ narakaṁ vrajet

That person who invites a poor alms-seeking brahmin, asks him many things, and then says it is not so, will go to hell permanently.

~

Interdependence among people living in a society is a necessity and a reality. Thus, due respect must be shown to those who may be in need of assistance for their well-being. Care should be exercised in making and keeping promises.

Heaven and Hell

Hindu mythology recognizes worlds above and below the earth. Specifically, the six worlds above the earth are the preferred ones for the soul and the seven below are to be feared. Thus, the lowest of the higher worlds is the earth (bhū). The six worlds above the earth (bhū) are called bhuva, suva, maha, jana, tapa, satya. The highest, not surprisingly, is the abode of Brahma the Creator and is known as the World of Truth (*Satya Loka*) reached after successfully passing through the hierarchy of worlds as the result of living a purer and purer life on earth.

Below the earth are the seven hells called talā-atala, bitala, sutala, talātala, rasātala, mahātala and pātāla. These hells are inhabited by those who need to undergo suffering based on the level of their condemnable actions while on earth. The lowest is considered an abode of demons and serpents and is reached successively through a hierarchy of hells due to worsening lives on earth birth after birth.

It should be understood that these mythological worlds are within the realm of ignorance. When a person understands his true nature of being Brahman, the Absolute, all sense of limitation dissolves. In other words, there are no worlds to negotiate in *mokshā*.

Asks the Yaksha:

राजन् कुलेन वृत्तेन स्वाध्यायेन शृतेन वा
ब्राह्मण्यं केन भवति? प्रब्रूह्येतत्सुनिश्चितं

rājan kulena vṛttena svādhyāyena śrutena vā
brāhmaṇyaṁ kena bhavati prabrūhyetatsu niścitaṁ

King, how does one become a brahmin, asks Yaksha next. Is it by birth? By conduct? By study of the Vedas? By education? Tell me precisely.

Yudhishthira replies:

शृणु यक्ष कुलं तात न स्वाध्यायो न च शृतं
कारणं हि द्विजत्वे च वृत्तमेव न संशयः

śruṇu yakṣa kulaṁ tāta nasvādhyāyo nacaśrutaṁ
kāraṇaṁ hi dvijatve ca vṛttameva na saṁśayaḥ

Listen, Yaksha, says Yudhishthira in reply to Yaksha's question, there is no doubt about it: it is not birth, it is not education, it is not even the study of the Vedas but it is conduct (character) alone that determines a brahmin thereon.

~

It is most illuminating to note Yudhishthira's emphasis of one's conduct as the determinant of being a brahmin.* He has already answered the same question in an earlier passage in the *Mahabharata* in his dialogue with King Nahusha: "He is known as a brahmin . . . in whom truthfulness, liberality, patience, mild deportment, self control, and compassion are found. And he may gain knowledge of the Supreme Brahman, beyond happiness and unhappiness . . . on reaching which they grieve no more."

* This inquiry and answer ought to be adequate to clear the great disagreement debate and disagreement in regard to caste. Swami Vivekananda in his lecture *(The Complete Works of Swami Vivekananda*, Advaita Ashram, Calcutta. Vol. 3, p. 197) on "The Mission of the Vedanta" declared that "Our ideal is the Brahmin of the spiritual culture and renunciation . . . I mean the Brahmin idealness in which worldliness is altogether absent and true wisdom is abundantly present. That is the ideal of the Hindu race."

Ask the Yaksha:	***Yudhishthira replies :***
प्रियवचनवादी किं लभते विमृशितकार्यकर: किं लभते बहुमित्रकर: किं लभते धर्मरत: किं लभते	प्रियवचनवादी प्रियोभवति विमृशितकार्य करोऽधिकं जयति बहुमित्र कर: सुखं वसते यश्चधर्मरत: स गतिं लभते
priyavacanavādī kiṁ labhate	*priyobhavati*
vimṛśita kāryakaraḥ kiṁ labhate	*adhikaṁ jayati*
bahumitrakaraḥ kiṁ labhate	*sukhaṁ vasate*
dharmarataḥ kiṁ labhate	*gatiṁ labhate*
What do soft-spoken people gain?	The love of all.
What do work-oriented people gain?	Success.
What do those who have many friends gain?	Happiness.
What do the dharmic people gain?	The ultimate goal.

~

These are pointed questions, and Yudhishthira's answers are valuable for all times. What is our goal? Do we wish to have many friends? Do we wish to be successful? Do we want to be happy? To be dharmic? Of course, we all do! And Yudhishthira's answers are precise and clear.

They draw a positive picture, a model for social and spiritual success:

1. Speak pleasantly of and with others (do not slander).
2. Work hard and with skill (do not be ignorant).
3. Make good friends and share with them (do not be greedy).
4. Be true to ourselves and to the highest goal of Self-realization.

Asks the Yaksha:

को मोदते

ko modate

Who is happy?

Yudhishthira replies:

पञ्चमेऽहनि षष्टे वा
शाकं पचति स्वे गृहे
अनृणानि चाप्रवासिच
स वारिचर मोदते

pañcamehani ṣaṣṭhe vā
śakaṁ pacati svegṛhe
anṛṇāni cāpravāsica
sa vāricara modate

The person who is free of debt, not in constant travel and who eats a frugal, satisfying hot meal in his own home every evening, such is a happy person.*

* Author's note: The translation of this last quartet of riddles is based largely on the graceful transcreation of the same passage in the poet P. Lal's *Mahabharata* (Writers Workshop, Calcutta).

Asks the Yaksha:

किमाश्चर्यं

kimāścaryaṁ?

What is amazing?

Yudhishthira replies:

अहन्यहनि भूतानि
गच्छंतीह यमालयं
शेषः स्थावरमिच्छंति
किमाश्चर्यमितः परं

ahanyahani bhūtāni
gacchaṁtīha yamālayaṁ
śeṣaḥ sthāvaramicchanti
kimāścaryamitaḥ paraṁ

Every day creatures die and yet everyone thinks
he lives for ever!
What can be more amazing and ironical?

~

Asks the Yaksha:

कः पंथाः

kaḥ panthāḥ

What is the path?

Yudhishthira replies:

तर्को अप्रतिष्ठः श्रुतयो विभिन्ना
नैको ऋषिर्यस्य मतं प्रमाणं
धर्मस्य तत्वं निहितं गुहायां
महाजनो येनगतः सपंथाः

tarko apratiṣṭhaḥ śrutayo vibhinnā
naiko ṛṣiryasya mataṁ pramāṇaṁ
dharmasya tatvaṁ nihitaṁ guhāyāṁ
mahājano yenagataḥ sapanthāḥ

What great men have followed — That is the path one must take,
because arguments are futile,
the Vedas are complex and different,
no single saint has the whole truth,
and the truth of dharma is mysteriously hidden.

~

Asks the Yaksha:

का च वार्तिका

kā ca vārtikā

What is happening?

Yudhishthira replies:

अस्मिन् महामोहमये कटाहे
सूर्याग्निना रात्रि दिवेंधनेन
मासर्तुदर्वी परिघट्टनेन
भूतानि कालः पचतीति वार्ता

asmin mahāmohamaye kaṭāhe
sūryāgninā rātri diveṁdhanena
māsartudarvī parighaṭṭanena
bhūtāni kālaḥ pacatīti vārtā

Time! It's relentless passage! That's what is happening.
In this massively deluded
cauldron of the world,
where the sun is fire
and the days and nights

fuel for that fire,
and the months and seasons
the ladle of the cauldron,
Time cooks creatures.
That's what's happening.

~

These questions are short, simple and direct, but not easy to answer. Their relevance is, of course, timeless. They have the character of what Mortimer Adler* calls "recurrent basic questions which men must face."**

The pursuit of happiness, as so many of these questions testify to was a major goal of ancient Indians. The answer, as always, the obvious one. It is rooted in simplicity and a mind at peace with itself.

The facts are that time passes and so do the mortal lives of living beings.

After all efforts and all learning, including the Vedas, the real guide is the example of those great and good among us who have successfully upheld dharma.

---

* *Great Ideas from the Great Books,* Wastington Sqaure Press, 1963, p.120.

** Author's note: The translation of this last quartet of riddles is based largely on the graceful transcreation of the same passage in the poet P. Lal's *Mahabharata* (Writers Workshop, Calcutta)

Asks the Yaksha:

व्याख्यातामे त्वया प्रश्ना याथातथ्यं परंतप
पुरुषं त्विदानो व्याख्याहि यश्च सर्वधनी नरः

vyākhyātā me tvayā praśnā yāthātathyaṁ paraṁtapa
puruṣaṁ tvidāno vyākhyāhi yaśca sarvadhanī naraḥ

You have answered all my questions correctly. But, now, explain further the following: What makes a man man? Which man has unlimited wealth?

Yudhishthira replies:

दिवं स्पृशति भूमिं च शब्दः पुण्येन कर्मणा
यावत्स शब्दो भवति तावत्पुरुष उच्यते

divaṁ spṛśati bhūmiṁ ca śabdaḥ puṇyena karmaṇā
yāvatsa śabdo bhavati tāvatpuruṣa ucyate

As long as one's fame reaches heaven and earth through one's good deeds that one will be called a man.

तुल्ये प्रियाप्रिये यस्य सुखदुःखे तथैव च
अतीतानागते चोभे स वै सर्वधनी नरः

tulye priyāpriye yasya sukhaduḥkhe tathaiva ca
atītānāgate cobhe sa vai sarvadhanī naraḥ

Whoever looks at the dualities (pleasant and unpleasant, joy and sorrow, past and future) the same way has all the wealth.

~

This concluding question and answer raises the level of discussion of Vedic Hindu culture up a few notches, setting up the stage for the yet to come philosophy enshrined in the *Bhagavad Gita*.

Vedas use the phrase *punya karma* for deeds done selflessly and detachedly in service of society. The implication here is that such service reaches the four corners of the world and the heavens. A brilliant contemporary example is that of Swami Vivekananda whose service to humanity will last till the end of time.

Unlimited wealth belongs to a *jnani* who has risen way above the limitations of body and mind, making no distinction between pain and pleasure, joy and sorrow, past and future. Fully present in the present moment, totally detached, free of thoughts of what happened before and what might happen later — such a person has no wants. He could not be wealthier!

An extraordinary standard! That, in the Hindu view, is the standard of excellence for mankind!

The stage is thus set for spiritual aspirants to lead a full life enriched with service to humanity in a totally detached but dynamic way. A welcome mat to enter the temple of *Srimad Bhagavad Gita*.

Epilogue

After listening to Yudhishthira's answers, the Yaksha declared himself very pleased and satisfied. He now wished to reward Yudhishthira for answering these difficult questions.

So the Yaksha said:

> त्वमेकं भ्रातृणाम् यमिच्छसि स जीवतु
>
> *tvamēkaṁ brātṛṇām yamicchasi sa jīvatu*
>
> One of your brothers can now be restored to life.
> The choice is yours!

So the test was not yet over! The Yaksha was not about to bring this whole episode to a happy ending by restoring all of Yudhishthira's four dead brothers to life. Not just yet. There remained one more agonizing question. Which among his brothers should or would Yudhishthira choose?

What a choice! To Yudhishthira all his brothers were precious. He equally loved Bhima, Arjuna, Nakula and Sahadeva. Arjuna had even gone to Indra's heaven to gather irresistible weapons and train for that terrible upcoming event, the great war between the Pandavas and Kauravas. Bhima's incredible strength was legendary, as was his ferocious loyalty, and his terrible vow to kill all the hundred Kauravas.

Is it all over for Yudhishthira? Even with four brave and loving brothers and the support of a few friendly kings, he had had only a slim chance to recover his legitimate share of the kingdom. Now he was all alone and was being asked to choose any one to be his sole surviving brother.

Does the Yaksha have no heart? Is he not fully satisfied by Yudhishthira's answers? Is he still not impressed by his impeccable character? Hasn't the eldest Pandava just displayed exemplary wisdom in answering with utmost care and clarity the most testing of Yaksha's questions? Is that all he now gets: a drink of water to quench his thirst and a solitary brother restored to life? Is there no compassion? No justice?

We might think thus, but Yudhishthira did not hesitate even for a moment. He said:

यक्ष नकुलो जीवतु

yaksha nakulō jīvatu

Yaksha, restore Nakula to life.

The Yaksha was astonished.

Incredulously he asked, "Why do you choose Nakula? He is only your step-brother! Bhima is your dear brother! Then, too, your whole security, your whole future depends upon the prowess of Arjuna. Why do you not choose either Bhima or Arjuna? Why Nakula?"

Yudhishthira's reply to the Yaksha at this point is most moving. What he said then regarding dharma is so vital, so fundamental, and so basic that it serves even now as a capstone of Hindu philosophy.

Yudhishthira simply said:

> धर्मो रक्षति रक्षितः
>
> *dharmō rakṣati rakśitaḥ*
>
> Those who protect dharma are protected by it.

Yudhishthira thus argued that to him both Kunti and Madri were equally his mothers. Therefore, at least one of Madri's sons should survive, just as he, Yudhishthira, a son of Kunti would. That, according to Yudhishthira would be dharma.

The Yaksha was pleased. Yudhishthira had now passed his final, perhaps the most difficult, test. He had upheld dharma. Whereupon, the Yaksha immediately restored to life all the four dead brothers. The brothers rose up looking hale and healthy and as if they were waking up from a long, restful sleep. Yudhishthira was overjoyed and embraced them all.

But Yudhishthira was now curious. He asked the Yaksha, "Who are you? You have to be a deva to have put to death these strong brothers of mine and restored them to life thus. You couldn't be a mere Yaksha."

Upon hearing this, the Yaksha admitted that he was none other than Yudhishthira's divine father, Yama Dharma, lord and judge of the dead. He also revealed that it was he who took the form of a deer and ran away with the brahmin's fire-drilling sticks. The father had come to test his son's strength of character and his adherence to dharma. Yama wanted to be sure that Yudhishthira still held steadfast to dharma even after twelve rigorous years of tough exile in forests. He also wanted to ascertain if Yudhishthira had developed the leadership skills needed to resolve the conflict between the Pandavas and the Kauravas.

Now convinced of Yudhishthira's strength, he granted him boons and asked him to choose whatever he wanted.

The first boon Yudhishthira asks of his father is that he return the fire-drilling sticks to the brahmin.

"Granted. The second boon?"

Yudhishthira then asks his father to bless the Pandavas so that they may not be detected during their last year of exile.

"Granted. One more boon?"

One would think that Yudhishthira would use this third boon to obtain assured success in the terrible battle looming ahead between the Pandavas are likely to have to fight against the Kauravas to regain their legitimate share of the empire. But, no! This son of Dharma, had other victories in mind. Yudhishthira said:

> जयेयं लोभमोहौ च क्रोधं चाहं सदा विभो
> दाने तपसि सत्ये च मनो मे सततं भवेत्
>
> *jayeyaṁ lobhamohau ca krodhaṁ cāhaṁ sadā vibho*
> *dāne tapasi satyeca mano me satataṁ bhavet*
>
> Grant me to be victorious over greed, folly, anger and to focus on charity, tapascharya (immersion in the self) and truth!

Incredible! This young man Dharmaputra is fighting altogether another war! His focus is inwards! His logic, perhaps, is that with the victory he is now seeking, other victories would inevitably follow!

Yudhishthira's request delighted his father even more. The test was now finally complete. Yama advised the five brothers to proceed forthwith to the kingdom of Virata to spend their thirteenth and final year of exile, and disappeared. The Pandavas, happy with the outcome of this quest, returned to their hermitage and began preparations to move on.

~

One might rightly wonder where and how the warrior prince Yudhishthira had gained the insights that enabled him to answer Yaksha's seemingly simple but truly complex questions covering a wide spectrum of beliefs deeply rooted in Hindu philosophy. The traumatic experience of public humiliation at the hands of Kauravas in the presence of elders in the family, the shameful treatment of his dear wife and princess by the evil cousin Dushasana, the loss of all his power and possessions, the years of imposed exile . . . the years of struggling to convince his wife and brothers to accept their difficult situation as part of an agreed-upon contract and higher purpose . . . all had tended to bring extraordinary focus on the deeper meaning of life.

Further, in the course of those twelve years the brothers and Draupadi traversed many forests and jungles through the length and breadth of India, and the hermitages of saints. They met many a great scholar and sage and were visited by many more. During the course of these visits, Yudhishthira had many opportunities to ask penetrating questions about his past and future fate, his destiny and purpose. Those dialogues and discourses evidently laid a foundation for all the wisdom that he displayed during the encounter with the Yaksha. This dialogue also lays the foundation for the more famous, complex and far-reaching exposition on dharma and *moksha* to come between Lord Krishna and Yudhishthira's brother Arjuna on the actual field of battle: the *Bhagavad Gita*. As a result the Hindu world is richer for it, and Ved Vyasa further promises:

इदं समुत्थान समागतं महत्
पितुः च पुत्रस्य च कीर्तिवर्धनं
पठन्नरः स्याद् विजीतेन्द्रियो वशी
सपुत्रपौत्रः शतवर्षभाग्भवेत्

idam samutthāna samāgatammahat
pituḥca putrasya ca kīrtivardhanaṁ
paṭhannaraḥ syād vijītendriyo vaśī
saputrapautrḥ śatavarṣa bhāg bhavet

Whoever recites or listens to this story of the dialogue
between the father and son will attain fame,
control of passions, be blessed with children
and grandchildren and a life of a hundred years.

Glossary

Adi Parva: Literally, "the starting book," the first book of the epic, the *Mahabharata.*

Aditya: Son of infinity or the endless heaven, personified by Aditi, a goddess. Here it refers to the sun.

Agnihotri: One who offers a fire sacrifice, an offering poured into *agni* (fire).

Antigod: A danava or child of the goddess Danu, an asura, a class of divine beings or demons opposed to the gods (*devas*); compare the titans of Greek mythology and their relationship to the Olympian gods.

Aranya Parva: Literally, "forest book," the third book of the *Mahabharata* which relates the adventures of the Pandavas during their exile in the forest.

Arjuna: Famous archer and warrior, the third son of Pandu by his queen Kunti. His divine father was Indra, King of heaven and wielder of the thunderbolt.

Artha: Object, matter, material wealth or purpose.

Atharva Veda: One of the four principal Vedas which form the *shruti* (revealed wisdom), the most sacred Hindu scriptures.

Ātman: The individual imperishable soul.

Bhagavadgita: Literally "the Song of God." This section of the epic, the *Mahabharata,* contains the dialogue between Prince Arjuna and his charioteer, Lord Krishna, Prince of Dwaraka, which has been given as high a sanction as the Vedas in modern Hinduism.

Bhagavad Gita: See *Bhagavadgita*.

Bhagavan, Bhagawan: God-like. variant spelling of Bhagavan used as a name of God, or as a title of respect.

Bharata: Ancestor of the Kauravas and Pandavas. Bharata Varsha was formerly a name given to Northern India.

Bhima: Son of Kunti, second of the Pandavas princes and famous for his incredible strength and ferocity in battle. His spiritual father was Vayu, the wind god.

Brahma: Pronounced 'Bram-ha', the Creator God and member — with Vishnu and Shiva — of an all powerful divine triad.

Brahman: The Supreme Principle of Life, the Paramatman or Over-Soul, which pervades all things; "Though men call it by many names, it is really One." (*Rig Veda).*

Brahmin: Traditionally the highest caste and socially considered a hereditary status. Brahmins have functioned as priests, scholars and expounders of the Vedas. Vyasa and other Upanishadic writers did not consider this social verdict as a moral law. Historically, in legend and through sanyas, the truly devout or brilliant have managed to flout it. As this text and other discourses throughout the *Mahabharata* emphasize, this status could be attained and should be maintained by strength of character (vritta) alone.

Deva: God

Dharma: Right course of conduct.

Dharmaraja: A title of Yudhishthira, who is considered an example of a just and upright ruler. He was also the spiritual son of Yama, often called Yama Dharma, the divine Judge.

Draupadi: Beautiful and spirited daughter of Drupada, King of Panchala. At her *swayamvara,* the assembly at which a princess could choose a husband, she chose Arjuna but finally became the wife of all the Pandavas.

Duryodhana: Eldest of the Kauravas, the hundred sons of Pandu's brother, the blind King Dhritarashtra. His ambition to gain the throne and his consuming jealousy of his cousins led him to the path of evil.

Gandharva: Minor deity, heavenly musician and singer.

Gandiva: The famous bow of Arjuna which brought lasting fame to the owner. Its lengthy history is told in the *Virata Parva* of the *Mahabharata.* Brahma was its first owner and it came eventually to Arjuna from Agni after the burning of the Khandava forest.

Ghee: Clarified butter; a major ingredient in ritual fire offerings.

Gita: See *Bhagavadgita.*

Havana: Sacrificial fire; the word is related to "oven" in English.

Hindu: Originally used to describe any inhabitant of India, the land beyond the river Indus (Sindhu), this word now used to describe a follower of Hinduism.

Hinduism: A major world religion originating in India, properly called Sanatana Dharma.

Homa: An oblation, a sacrificial pouring into fire.

Jyoti: Light.

Kama: Desire, matters of the senses; sometimes personified as Kama (the Indian Cupid or Eros).

Kannada: A South Indian language, used in the state of Karnataka; and belonging to the Dravidian family of languages.

Karma: Action.

Kaurava: Son or descendant of Kuru.

Kshatriya: The warrior caste, whose principal duty is the defense of the country: ranked as second function in traditional Hinduism.

Kunti: Daughter of Sura of the Yadava clan, she was adopted by Kuntibhoja and later married to Pandu. Thanks to a boon she was able to overcome a curse against Pandu which prevented him from having children. She bore three sons, by three different gods, to Pandu and helped his second queen, Madri, to bear twin sons. Her original name was Pritha and her sons are often addressed as "Kaunteya," son of Kunti, or "Partha," son of Pritha.

Kuru: Ancestor of the sons of Pandu and the sons of Dhritarashtra. The epithet "Kaurava" in the *Mahabharata* is usually reserved for Duryodhana and his ninety-nine brothers.

Kurukshetra: The field of battle, north of the modern city of New Delhi, where the sons of Pandu fought with their cousins, the 100 sons of Dhritarashtra.

Madri: Sister of the King of Madra and second wife of Pandu. Thanks to Kunti, she was able to bear twin sons after invoking the heavenly horsemen, the twin Ashwins. She immolated herself on Pandu's funeral pyre and her children were raised by Kunti. Yudhishthira's respect for Madri and love for his twin brothers helped him pass the Yaksha's final test. Madri's sons were often addressed as "Madreya," son of Madri.

Mahabharata: One of the major Hindu epics, this is the great *(maha)* story of the princes of the racc of Bharata and their quarrel which extended into a war between good and evil, right and wrong, for the sake of dharma. It contains the *Bhagavadgita,* the dialogue between Arjuna and Krishna, which is often read for its own sake.

Marut: Minor troop-deity, a wind god.

Moksha: Spiritual salvation; release from rebirth and the wheel of time.

Nahusha: A king cursed by the sage Agastya to live as a serpent until Yudhishthira came to answer his questions on ethics.

Nakula: One of the twin sons of Madri and Pandu, one of the 5 Pandavas. He was noted for his handsome appearance and skill in horsemanship.

Nara: Man, human being.

Navagrahas: The "Nine Planets" of Vedic astrology: Surya (Sun), Chandra (Moon), Angaraka or Mangala (Mars), Budha (Mercury), Brihaspati or Guru (Jupiter), Shukra (Venus), Rahu (lunar mode; eclipse), Ketu (lunar mode, comet).

Om: Sometimes spelled "*aum*" a sound-syllable or mantra for God.

Pandava: Son of Pandu.

Pandu: Prince of the Kuru clan and descendant of Bharata. Since he could not have children of his own, his wife Kunti used a boon, earned from the sage Durvasa while she was a child, to obtain three sons, Yudhishthira, Bhima and Arjuna, for herself and twin sons, Nakula and Sahadeva, for Pandu's second wife. Pandu was noted for his pale complexion, prowess in battle and generosity of temperament.

Parva: One of the eighteen major sections of the *Mahabharata*.

Peetham: Seat, site.

Pitṛ: Literally, "father," ancestor.

Prashna: Questions.

Purana: A story of gods, sages and mythological heroes, mixed with traditional lore. The puranas, along with the epics, the *Ramayana* and the *Mahabharata,* form that body of Hindu scripture called *smriti* or remembered wisdom.

Rakshasa: Demon.

Rig Veda: The oldest extant religious text in the world, dating back at least to 3000 B.C. It contains 1,017 hymns in 10 books.

Rishis: Ancient and powerful sages, seven or twelve in number. They include Gautama, Bharadvaja, Vishwamitra, Vashishta, Kashyapa, Marichi, Jamadagni, Atri, Bhrigu, Agastya and others. Although human in form, they have divine powers and are incarnated from one age to another.

Rudra: A name of Shiva and also minor troop deity, a storm god.

Sabha Parva: Literally "council book," second book of the *Mahabharata*, containing the ill-fated Dice Game which leads to the exile of the Pandavas.

Sahadeva: Second of the twin sons of Madri; famous, like his brother Nakula, for his good looks and skill with horses and cattle.

Sama Veda: One of the four principal Vedas; it contains the Chandogya Upanishad.

Sanskrit: Oldest existing member of the Indo-European family of languages to which English itself as well as many modern Indian languages, such as Hindi, belong.

Sanyasi(n): A person dedicated to a monastic life of celibacy, poverty and obedience to the rules of a religious order; such a person may spend time in prayer, study of the expounding of the scriptures or meditation.

Savitri: Wife of Satyavan, saved her husband from death by outwitting Yama. Her story, a well known example of wifely devotion and woman's wit, is given in the *Mahabharata*.

Shanti: Variant spelling, 'shanthi', means peace. Combined with the syllable *om* repeated three times "*Om shanti shanti shantihi*" it is a common benediction or conclusion to a recitation of prayer, close in meaning to the biblical phrase, "Peace unto you."

Shloka: Strophe or verse stanza.

Srimad Bhagavadgita: See *Bhagavad Gita*.

Svadharma: One's own dharma or set of chosen principles.

Swami: Means lord, master used as a title for religious leader.

Tapasya: Penance, sacrifice, mode of self-discipline.

Taittiriya Brahmana: A branch of Krishna Yajurveda dealing with sacrifices such as, for example, in context, Agnihotra

Upanishads: Metaphysical discourses which form the speculative body of wisdom attached to the four Vedas. There are over 200 texts called Upanishads, but only about fourteen are considered as belonging to the shruti or genuine revealed scriptures. They include the Isha, Kena, Katha, Prashna, Mundaka, Mandukya, Taittiriya, Aitareya, Chandogya, Brihadaranyaka, Kaushitaki, Maitrayaniya, and Shvetashvatara.

Vasu: A class of minor deities, the "good ones."

Ved Vyasa: Compiler and author of the epic, the *Mahabharata*, which has been popularly called the fifth Veda. By his own account he was the son of the sage Parashara and Satyavati who later married King Shantanu, grandfather of the Kauravas and Pandavas.

Veda: More often referred to as the Vedas, four in number: *Rig Veda*, *Yajur Veda*, *Atharva Veda* and *Sama Veda*. Each is divided into hymns (samhita), rituals and formulas (brahmanas) and metaphysical discourses on the themes of the hymns (aranyakas and upanishads). These collectively form a body of scripture known as *shruti* or revealed wisdom which has the highest authority in Hinduism. The word veda means wisdom and has been translated as "beginningless knowledge" (Alain Danielou, *Hindu Polytheism,* p. 200).

Vedanta: A metaphysical system of thought based on the Vedas and Upanishads.

Vedic: Pertaining to the Vedas.

Virata Parva: Literally "book of Virata," fourth book of the Mahabharata, containing the adventures of the Pandavas and Draupadi during the thirteenth year of exile which was spent in disguise at the court of King Virata.

Vivekananda: (1863-1902) follower of Sri Ramakrishna Paramahamsa, founded the Vedanta Societies of America and Europe. He first visited the United States in 1893 as a delegate to the World Parliament of Religions at the Columbian Exposition in Chicago. He wrote and lectured extensively during his short lifetime and is one of the great saints of modern Hinduism.

Vritta: Moral strength of character.

Yajna: Ritual sacrifice, as opposed to *puja* which is individual worship. Sometimes written as yagna, close to a common pronunciation.

Yajur Veda: One of the four principal Vedas. It contains the Katha, Isha and Brihadaranyaka Upanishads.

Yaksha: A minor deity, a sprite or earth spirit.

Yama: Lord and judge of the dead, arbiter of divine justice. He is the spiritual father of Yudhishthira.

Yudhishthira: Son of Kunti and eldest of Pandu sons; a staunch upholder of dharma, a man of compassion, grace, tact and high principles.

Yuga: Era: specifically the four yugas which form an age in the history of the world; Krita (Satya) Yuga, Treta Yuga, Dwapara Yuga and Kali Yuga.

Appendix

Yaksha's Questions and Yudhishthira's Answers

1. What makes the sun rise?
   — Brahma.
2. Who moves around him?
   — Gods.
3. What causes the sun to set?
   — Dharma.
4. In what is he established?
   — Truth.
5. How does one become a scholar?
   — By study of the Vedas.
6. How does one become exalted?
   — Through tapas.
7. How does one gain a second self?
   — With resolve.
8. How does one become wise?
   — By serving the elders.

9. What marks divinity in brahmins?
   — Vedic knowledge.

10. What laws of theirs do the good share?
    — Tapasya.

11. What is their human attribute?
    — Mortality.

12. What makes them resemble the unworthy?
    — Slander.

13. What marks divinity in the kshatriyas?
    — Skill in arms.

14. What practice do they (the kshatriyas) share with the good?
    — Yajnas.

15. What is their human attribute?
    — Fear.

16. When do they resemble the unworthy?
    — Abandoning the distressed.

17. What makes the chant of a yajna?
    — Prāna.

18. What makes the yaju (sacrifice) of a yajna?
    — Mind.

19. What makes the refuge of a yajna?
    — *Rig Veda.*

20. Without what is there no yajna?
    — *Rig Veda.*

21. What remains most beneficial even when it's falling?
— Rain.

22. What remains most beneficial even when it's thrown down?
— Seeds.

23. What is most sought by property seekers?
— Cattle.

24. What is most desirable for those seeking progeny?
— Sons.

25. Is there a person who enjoys all pleasures of the senses, who is intelligent, is respected by all creatures and worshipped by the world, who breathes and yet is not alive?
— The person who fails to satisfy gods, guests, servants, *pitṛs* and his *ātman* may breathe but is not alive.

26. What is weightier than earth?
— Mother.

27. What is taller than the sky?
— Father.

28. What is faster than the wind?
— Mind.

29. What is more numerous than grass?
— Thoughts.

30. What sleeps with its eyes open?
— A fish.

31. What remains still even after birth?
— An egg.

32. What has no heart?
— A stone.

33. What swells quickly by itself?
— A river.

34. Who is the traveler's friend?
— A companion.

35. Who is the householder's friend?
— A spouse.

36. Who is the friend of the sick?
— A doctor.

37. Who is the friend of the dying?
— His charity.

38. Who is the guest of all creatures?
— Agni.

39. What is the eternal dharma?
— Amrita.

40. What is amrita?
— Cow's milk.

41. What is this entire universe?
— Air.

42. What moves about alone?
— The sun.

43. Who, once born, is born again?
    — The moon.

44. What is the remedy against mist?
    — Fire (agni).

45. Which is the largest vessel?
    — Earth.

46. What in one word is dharma?
    — Skill.

47. What in one word is fame?
    — Charity.

48. What in one word is heaven?
    — Truth.

49. What in one word is happiness?
    — Character.

50. What is a man's self?
    — His progeny.

51. Who is his God-given friend?
    — His spouse.

52. What supports his life?
    — Rain.

53. What is the principal goal?
    — Charity.

54. Which treasure is the best?
    — Skill.

55. Which wealth is the best?
— Education.

56. What is the greatest gain?
— Health.

57. And the greatest happiness?
— Contentment.

58. What is the supreme dharma in the world?
— Non-maliciousness.

59. Which dharma always bears fruit?
— Vedic dharma.

60. By restraining what is one free from grief?
— Mind.

61. Between whom does a bond not wither?
— Good people.

62. By renouncing what does one become lovable?
— Pride.

63. By renouncing what is one free from sorrow?
— Anger.

64. By renouncing what does one become wealthy?
— Desire.

65. By renouncing what does one become happy?
— Greed.

66. Why is one charitable to brahmins?
— For the sake of dharma.

67. Why does one support actors, dancers?
— To gain renown.

68. Why does one give to those who serve us?
— For their livelihood.

69. Why does one pay (taxes) to kings?
— Out of fear.

70. What engulfs the world?
— Ignorance.

71. What prevents the world from illumination?
— Spiritual darkness.

72. Why does one forsake friends?
— Greed.

73. What limits one's attainment of heaven?
— Attachment.

74. What makes a man dead?
— (When) he is poor.

75. What makes a nation dead?
— (When) it's without a ruler.

76. What makes a shrāddha dead?
— (When) led by the ignorant.

77. What makes a yajnā dead?
— When no gift is offered.

78. What is the direction (one should take)?
— The way of the good.

79. What are water, food and poison?
— Sky, cow's products, begging.

80. What is the right time for a shrāddha?
— A learned brahmin's time.

81. What constitutes impeccability?
— Following one's own dharma.

82. What is discipline?
— Restraint of one's mind.

83. What is forbearance?
— Tolerating opposites.

84. What constitutes a sense of shame?
— Backing away from unaccepted behavior.

85. What is knowledge?
— Cognition of the true nature of things.

86. What is tranquility?
— A serene mind.

87. What is the supreme compassion?
— Wishing the happiness of all.

88. What is simplicity?
— A poised mind.

89. Which enemy is nearly impossible to conquer?
— Anger.

90. What is man's endless disease?
— Greed.

91. Who is good?
— One who seeks the good of all.

92. Who is not good?
— One who lacks compassion.

93. What is delusion?
— Inability to grasp the essentials of dharma.

94. What is pride?
— An exaggerated sense of self-importance.

95. What is laziness?
— Not acting dharmically.

96. What is grief?
— Ignorance.

97. What do the sages call steadfastness?
— Being rooted in one's own dharma.

98. What is courage?
— Keeping one's senses in check.

99. What is the supreme cleansing?
— Cleansing of the mind.

100. What is charity?
— Protection of all creatures.

101. Who qualifies to be called wise?
— One who knows dharma.

102. Who is an atheist?
— Said to be a fool.

103. Who is a fool?
— One who is covetous.

104. What is desire?
— The cause of rebirth.

105. What is jealousy?
— Heartache.

106. What is egoism?
— Total ignorance of one's true nature.

107. What is hypocrisy?
— Pretending to be dharmic.

108. What is divine?
— Fruits of charity.

109. What is vice?
— Slandering others.

110. Dharma, artha and kama conflict with each other. How can these contraries be reconciled?
— When dharma and one's spouse are in harmony, dharma, artha and kama are reconciled.

111. How does one obtain permanent hell?
— That person who invites a poor alms-seeking brahmin, asks him many things, and then says it is not so, will go to hell permanently.

112. King, how does one become a brahmin? Is it by birth? by conduct? by study of the Vedas? by education? Tell me precisely.
— Listen, Yaksha, it is neither birth nor education, nor even the study of the Vedas. Without doubt, it is conduct (character) alone that determines a brahmin.

113. What do soft-spoken people gain?
— The love of all.

114. What do work-oriented people gain?
— Success.

115. What do those who have many friends gain?
— Happiness.

116. What do the dharmic people gain?
— The ultimate goal.

117. Who is happy?
— That person who is free of debt, not in constant travel and who eats a frugal, satisfying hot meal in his own home every evening, such is a happy person.

118. What is amazing?
— Every day creatures die and yet everyone thinks he lives for ever! What can be more amazing and ironical?

119. What is the path?
— What great men have followed — That is the path one must take, because arguments are futile, the Vedas are complex and different, no single saint has the whole truth and the truth of dharma is mysteriously hidden.

120. What is happening?
    — Time! It's relentless passage! That's what is happening.

121. What makes a man man?
    — As long as one's fame reaches heaven and earth through one's good deeds that one will be called a man.

122. Which man has unlimited wealth?
    — Whoever looks at the dualities (pleasant and unpleasant, joy and sorrow, past and future) the same way, has all the wealth.